# ORGANISING
# A CONFERENCE

*If you want to know how...*

**Presenting with Power**
*Captivate, motivate, inspire, persuade*

'All speakers will benefit from reading this excellent book.' –
Molly Harvey, Vice president of the Professional Speakers
Association

**Producing Successful Magazines, Newsletters and E-zines**

'This is a thoroughly useful publication for people who have
just been given the exciting challenge of producing the
company magazine.' – Communicators

**Writing a Report**
*How to prepare, write and present effective reports*

'...by far the most informative text covering report writing that
I have seen.' – Training Journal

**howto**books

Please send for a free copy of the latest catalogue:

How To Books
3 Newtec Place, Magdalen Road,
Oxford OX4 1RE, United Kingdom
email: info@howtobooks.co.uk
http://www.howtobooks.co.uk

# ORGANISING A CONFERENCE

How to plan and run a successful
and effective event

## Pauline Appleby

**how**tobooks

Published by How To Books Ltd,
3 Newtec Place, Magdalen Road,
Oxford OX4 1RE. United Kingdom.
Tel: (01865) 793806. Fax: (01865) 248780.
email: info@howtobooks.co.uk
http://www.howtobooks.co.uk

First edition 1999
Second edition 2002
Third edition 2005

British Library Cataloguing in Publication Data
A catalogue record for this book is available from the British
Library

Cover design by Baseline Arts Ltd, Oxford
Produced for How To Books by Deer Park Productions, Tavistock
Typeset by PDQ Typesetting, Newcastle-under-Lyme
Printed and bound by Cromwell Press, Trowbridge, Wiltshire

NOTE: The material contained in this book is set out in good
faith for general guidance and no liability can be accepted
for loss or expense incurred as a result of relying in particular
circumstances on statements made in the book. The laws and
regulations are complex and liable to change, and readers should
check the current position with the relevant authorities before
making personal arrangements.

# Contents

List of Illustrations                                              viii

Preface                                                             ix

1   **What is a Conference?**                                       **1**
    Understanding the reasons for conferences                       1
    Understanding the importance of communication                   3
    Planning your own conference                                    4

2   **Choosing a Venue**                                            **8**
    Looking at your options                                         8
    Making sense of the brochure                                    10
    Assessing venue-finding options                                 11
    Viewing a potential venue                                       12
    Assessing the facilities                                        13
    Establishing what is included                                   23

3   **Sourcing Speakers and Setting the Programme**                 **25**
    Conducting market research                                      25
    Designing a questionnaire                                       25
    Finding speakers                                                26
    Corresponding with speakers                                     30
    Understanding the role of the chairperson                       37

4   **The Conference Brochure**                                     **38**
    Designing the brochure                                          38
    Printing the brochure                                           41
    Distributing the brochure                                       42

5   **Working to a Schedule**                                       **44**
    Scheduling the event                                            44
    Creating a plan                                                 45
    Scheduling the programme                                        46

**6    Setting up a Registration System**                          **52**
Using computerised registration systems                         52
Web-based registration systems                                  53
Other registration options                                      54
Setting up your own in-house manual system                      55
Registering delegates on-site                                   58

**7    Planning Budgets and Sponsorship**                         **60**
Setting budgets                                                 60
Insuring against disasters                                      64
Controlling the catering costs                                  64
Negotiating rates                                               67
Arranging sponsorship                                           68
Taking care of sponsors                                         70

**8    Assessing the Audio Visual Requirements**                  **74**
Looking at the choice of visual projection                      74
Sound systems and related items                                 78
Operating the equipment                                         80
Contracting an audio visual company                             81

**9    Staging the Event**                                        **83**
Staffing the event                                              83
Before the day starts                                           84
Dealing with registration                                       85
Preparing delegate packs                                        87
Remembering delegate care                                       87
Remembering speaker care                                        91
Trouble-shooting                                                93

**10   Obtaining Press Coverage**                                 **94**
Selecting the appropriate media                                 94
Writing the press release                                       96
Looking after the journalists                                   98
Providing a press room                                          98
Post-conference publicity                                       99

**11   Exhibitors and Exhibitions**                              **100**
The exhibition industry                                        100
Incorporating an exhibition in your conference                 101
Sourcing exhibitors                                            102

|  | | |
|---|---|---|
| What to include in the cost | | 102 |
| Allocating space | | 103 |
| Making it worthwhile for exhibitors | | 106 |
| **12** | **The Morning After** | **108** |
| | Winding down | 108 |
| | Developing relationships | 109 |
| | Evaluating the event | 110 |
| | Where to go from here | 112 |
| Appendix 1 Data Protection | | 114 |
| Appendix 2 Health and Safety | | 117 |
| Appendix 3 First Aid | | 121 |
| Appendix 4 Booking Forms | | 123 |
| Appendix 5 Banquets/Conference Dinners | | 127 |
| Useful Addresses | | 131 |
| Index | | 133 |

# List of Illustrations

1. Communicating as conference manager      4
2. Venue checklist      14
3. Seating plans and room styles      16
4. Call for papers      29
5. Invitation to speaker      31
6. Speaker hints and tips      36
7. Time plan illustration (i)      47
8. Time plan illustration (ii)      48
9. Conference programme      49
10. Delegate confirmation letter      57
11. Example budget – projected      62
12. Example budget – actual      62
13. Finding the break-even point      63
14. Sponsorship opportunity form      71
15. Sponsorship confirmation letter      72
16. Audio visual request form      82
17. Tool box contents list      92
18. Press release      98
19. Evaluation form      111
20. Risk assessment form      126

# Preface

I recently attended a planning meeting for a large conference to be run by a national charity. In addition to the national conference in which I was to be involved, each of the regional managers was also to organise a smaller conference in their own region. The questions they asked me in relation to their individual events were ones commonly asked by people in similar positions, i.e. those required to organise a conference for which they have little or no experience.

This guide is written with those people in mind. It may be that having read it you become aware of how much work is involved and either decide that you do have the time, ability and resources available to do it yourself, or identify it as a project to be out-sourced. A common result is for a combination of these two outcomes, where some elements of the organisational task are handled in-house, whilst others are out-sourced to professionals.

Of course, all organisers have their own way of doing things and the message must be to find what works for you and to learn by all of your experiences, be they as a delegate or as an organiser.

In earlier editions I acknowledged the help and advice of the following: Monica Allen, Jayne Buckland, Caroline Hannon, Deborah Delord, Tracy Johnson, Malcolm Thompson (MC Productions) and Peter Worger (ACE).

For this third edition I would like to add to that list all of the Health Links team and Tom Ashton.

Lastly, not only do I hope you will find this guide useful, but also that you enjoy what you do.

*Pauline Appleby*

# What is a Conference?

*'The Oxford Dictionary defines a conference as a meeting for discussion.'*

## UNDERSTANDING THE REASONS FOR CONFERENCES

Conferences are sometimes also called seminars, which are usually smaller groups of delegates, or symposiums – a conference or meeting to discuss a particular subject. Whatever the title, and whatever the subject, one thing is instrumental to them all: that is *communication*.

From the local gardening club to the richest charities, from trade associations to multinational companies, all will have their own agenda and reason for running a conference. It could be:

♦ for fund-raising
♦ to raise awareness
♦ to share information
♦ a learning forum
♦ a promotional event
♦ to bring together members or employees spread throughout the country or overseas.

Very different reasons and very different organisations, but there are many elements of the organisation process of the event that will be similar in each case.

## Knowing who runs conferences

Some organisations employ dedicated conference staff, often within an events department, trained by staff experienced in event management. This is often the case if the organisation runs several events each year as part of the company's overall marketing strategy. Freelance professional conference organisers may be contracted-in to increase manpower when required. Alternatively, in these days of short-term contracts and tendering, an organisation may contract-out all of their event management to a freelance organiser or specialist company. This can be beneficial to the company as a cost-effective option allowing the company to concentrate on its core skills and objectives.

However in many, particularly smaller, organisations, charities, societies and clubs, the responsibility for putting together the conference is often delegated to an untrained and inexperienced person, committee member or marketing assistant who is expected to take on the workload whilst carrying out their normal job.

A well run conference belies the amount of work that is carried out in preparation.

Indeed the task can be a daunting one, and there are many pitfalls, but with guidance it can be done. A well organised event can have a great impact on the stakeholders, be they paying delegates, invited guests, speakers, members of the press, in-house staff, etc, but a badly organised event can have a disastrous effect which will be remembered for a long time. Many professional conference organisers originally came into the industry 'unintentionally' having been asked to run their first conference whilst working in other roles. Having enjoyed it so much they then chose to make a career move into the industry.

## UNDERSTANDING THE IMPORTANCE OF COMMUNICATION

Communication is vital to society. Without communication we would have no chance of survival. The very fact that early man was a co-operative hunter means that they must have been able to communicate in one way or another. A baby communicates its feelings of hunger by crying, a board of directors communicates with shareholders by written communication, a mute person communicates using hand signals. To impart information of any kind we need to find the method of communication appropriate to our circumstances.

Conferences are all about communication – be it to sell, to inform, to enthuse, to entertain, or to educate.

### Types of communication

Many different methods of communication are used. The first we normally think of is of course verbal, but the first communication you have with a delegate will probably be in the form of written words. During the event itself messages will be received, sometimes subliminally, by the delegates through:

◆ logos
◆ diagrams
◆ banners

◆ body language (facial expressions, body posture and gestures).

As the conference manager you must be aware of the need for good communication skills. Think of all the people you will be interacting with. A few are shown in Figure 1.

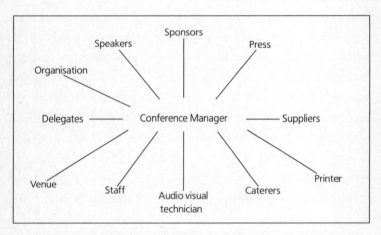

Fig. 1. Communicating as conference manager.

### How you already interact

You will already be communicating with many people in your own organisation, whether they are work colleagues or fellow society members. Think about the various groups who you interact with on a regular basis. Try drawing a diagram as Figure 1, and include as many groups as possible and list below each which types of communication you may use. You will be surprised at how many there are and so how practised you must already be!

## PLANNING YOUR OWN CONFERENCE

Conferences can be customised to your own specific

requirements. They can last for a whole day, half a day, a weekend, an evening, two days or more. The word 'conference' merely describes the nature of the event. The content, duration and outcome of it can be entirely at your discretion. Although you may feel more confident following someone else's example at your first event, feel free to be imaginative and creative. Conferences do not all have to consist of a panel of speakers addressing a totally passive audience. You could include debates, hands-on experiences, workshops and discussion groups. It can be kicked off with a sponsored breakfast and finished off with a gala dinner. You can incorporate a small exhibition, a competition or challenge of some kind, and utilise lighting, special effects and imaginative stage sets to increase the impact of the event.

**Individualising your conference**
Conferences can be held in hotels, on boats, in museums, or in purpose-built conference and training centres. They can be for half a dozen people or for thousands. They may be run in conjunction with a major exhibition, or they may be a conference first and foremost and include their own small exhibition. No two events are the same, not even when run by the same organisation on the same theme. The mix of speakers, organisers, delegates and supporting staff will combine to produce a different atmosphere every time. External events attracting media interest in a particular subject can vastly increase the popularity of the event if the interest is positive, or drastically affect its success if negative.

Fees charged for attending events vary enormously. Some

events are free of charge, whilst others may charge hundreds of pounds for a one-day event. Budgets may be huge, supported by big sponsorship deals, or it may be run on a shoe-string and be self-financing.

There may be one or two speakers, or there may be dozens. Speakers may be paid hundreds of pounds, or just expenses. Every organiser will have their own way of doing things, their own priorities and their own schedule. You will need to find what works for you.

### Benefits of a conference

♦ Provides an environment for networking.

♦ Provides a forum for discussion.

♦ Provides an opportunity to promote ideas/products/ beliefs.

♦ Creates a sense of belonging.

♦ Can enable learning and awareness.

### Checklist

♦ What resources are available to you and what happens if you need more?

♦ What are the limits of your responsibilities and what tasks can you delegate? Don't forget you can delegate authority but you cannot delegate responsibility.

♦ What can you, and what would you like to, do yourself?

♦ What do you need help to do?

- What contacts do you already have? Where can you find more?

- What help is available?

- How many different purposes can you list for your conference?

# 2

# Choosing a Venue

*'The more the organisers can do to create an
ideal learning environment the better.'*

## LOOKING AT YOUR OPTIONS

More often than not delegates will be attending a
conference in order to learn something and/or to
exchange information.

This does not mean the provision of schoolmasters and
blackboards, but an environment as comfortable and
distraction-free as possible. Delegates arriving after
perhaps a long and testing journey need to be able to
enter a calm atmosphere, and be able to relax and shut
out the outside world. The venue, its location, and the
demeanour of the conference and venue staff all have a
large part to play in this.

### Choosing the venue to suit your budget

Conference venues come in all shapes and sizes with
varying facilities and with equally varied budgets.

- ◆ Modern, purpose-built conference centres have the
  latest in audio visual equipment.

- ◆ Training centres belonging to large corporations are
  leased out when not in use.

- Country houses offer numerous outdoor activities within their grounds.

- Hotels have the benefit of overnight accommodation and sometimes leisure facilities for delegates.

If you are working on a tight budget, civic centres and council-owned buildings such as sports and leisure centres can be a very economical option. In these venues the charge is often based upon room hire cost and the catering is supplied by an outside caterer who retains a contract with the council. The facilities will vary from very basic sports halls to grand Victorian council chambers.

### Making use of universities

Universities offer a choice of conference facilities at a reasonable cost. These can vary from basic lecture theatres with hard wooden benches and graffiti-covered desks (thankfully more of a rarity these days) to state-of-the-art, purpose-built conference suites with individual cushioned seating. A major advantage of university facilities is that during the vacation periods the student accommodation can be booked at an extremely reasonable price. Again, the standard of this accommodation can vary enormously from university to university.

### Considering somewhere unusual

Other more unusual venues include football stadiums and race courses. Again, these often offer excellent value for money and due to the nature of their core business have superb car parking and dining facilities, and are often well signposted on roads in the surrounding area. Museums can also provide a venue with a difference. Having refreshments on a gallery overlooking a display of dinosaur skeletons can provide unexpected but much appreciated interest for the delegates, and their often tiered theatres can be of a very high standard.

> For a very unusual event, why not charter a boat and have your conference whilst floating sedately down a river?

## MAKING SENSE OF THE BROCHURE

Almost every conference facility will produce a leaflet or brochure describing their facilities to would-be organisers. Remember that the purpose of providing this information is to present the venue in the best possible light, so use the information purely as a guideline on which to base your further enquiries.

### Knowing what to look for

Whether you are booking a four star hotel, a leisure centre or a university complex the brochure should give you:

◆ contact information
◆ an overview of the venue itself
◆ room capacity according to layout required.

Use the information wisely – a room capacity of 100 delegates may be fine if front projection is being used, but for back projection that number could reduce dramatically. A hall advertised as being suitable for 200 delegates may appear at first glance to look perfect, until you realise that those delegates are going to have to share two toilets during the 15-minute coffee break.

♦ Use your brochure to short-list the venues that *appear* suitable.

## ASSESSING VENUE-FINDING OPTIONS
In every town there will be dozens of potential venues, with capacities varying from ten people to 1,000. So how do you know where to start looking?

### Venue-finding services
Professional venue-finding services can be found listed in *Yellow Pages* directories and in trade journals (see Further Reading). They can dramatically cut down the time and money you need to spend on making initial enquiries. The service is usually free as they are financed by commission payable when the client makes the booking. It is likely that they will have a wealth of knowledge about different types of venues, and will usually locate a selection of potential venues for you to view. Often they will arrange for a brochure to be sent to you and make appointments for viewing on your behalf.

### Considering the pros and cons of using a venue-finding service
♦ Sometimes the choice of venues on their books is limited to those who pay to be there, which can mean that the service may be biased.

♦ Venue-finding services will also often negotiate costs with venues on your behalf. They will already have a good idea of how far below the published delegate price a particular venue is likely to go.

### Venue-finding software

There are various software packages on the market, some of which are available free of charge, from which you can download onto your own computer a short-list of potentially suitable venues. Again these may be limited to the companies who pay to have their information included but the choice is extensive.

### Using a local council conference bureau

Most local councils now have dedicated conference departments, usually attached to the tourism bureau, whose job it is to attract conferences and events to their area. The standard of service varies enormously, from simply providing brochures to arranging hosted visits, arranging partner programmes and making hotel bookings. The staff can be less biased than privately run venue-finding services as they are not subject to private financing. The British Association of Conference Destinations produces an excellent handbook containing contact details of its members (see Useful Addresses).

No matter how suitable a venue looks from the brochure, do try to visit. Even if you will find it difficult finding the time to travel to another part of the country, it will be well worth making the effort. You could always take the train and work while you travel!

## VIEWING A POTENTIAL VENUE

It is essential to book an appointment before visiting a venue so that your point of contact is able to devote his/her time to you. Arrive a few minutes early to enable you to assess your own first impression of the facility. Imagine you are a delegate, entering for the first time. Remember that in the role of organiser you are going to get to know the building and staff very well before and during the event, but your delegates will pretty much take the venue at face value for their shortened stay.

*Observing the staff*
Sit back and observe how the staff interact with each other.

◆ Are they cheerful and respectful of one another, or is there underlying discontent?

◆ How are they dealing with other visitors to the venue?

Before you visit, draw up a list of the essential items that you will require for your particular event. These are items that cannot be compromised upon, however much you are impressed with the venue. Also take a checklist of general items, such as the one in Figure 2, so that you can later compare notes on the various venues you look at.

## ASSESSING THE FACILITIES

### Getting there
It may be the intention to take your delegates to a venue off the beaten track so that they are in serene surroundings with little to distract them but the glorious countryside all around. On the other hand, you may be expecting them to travel into a city from various regions of the country and back again on the same day, in which case ease of locating the venue will be of great importance. Consider the following factors:

# VENUE CHECKLIST

**Name of venue**
Ease of locating venue                    *Car parking*
*Conference room*
   ◆ style
   ◆ capacity
   ◆ ceiling height
*Toilets*
   ◆ number of cubicles for ladies
   ◆ disabled facilities
*Lighting*
   ◆ is there natural daylight?
   ◆ blackout facilities
   ◆ spotlights
   ◆ lectern lights
   ◆ location of control panel
*Chairs*
*Obstructions*
*Exhibition space*
   ◆ number and location of electricity sockets
   ◆ number and location of telephone points
   ◆ location in relation to conference
*Audio visual equipment*
   ◆ what does the hotel own?
   ◆ how much is included in the costs?
   ◆ what is the cost of hiring items from the venue?
   ◆ what condition is it in?
*Accommodation*
   ◆ what is the capacity?
   ◆ condition of rooms
   ◆ facilities provided in rooms, e.g. hairdryers, TV, trouser press, skirt
     hangers, air conditioning
*Catering*
   ◆ selection of sample menus
   ◆ what is included in cost?
   ◆ how much do additional teas/coffees, etc cost?
   ◆ will lunch be taken standing up or sitting down?
   ◆ will lunch be served in the room or elsewhere?

*Cloakroom facilities*

*Pay phone*

*Charges*
   ◆ day delegate rate
   ◆ 24-hr rate
   ◆ room hire rate (if applicable)
   ◆ deposit required
   ◆ will venue negotiate?
   ◆ what is the deadline for cancellation and what is the cancellation
     policy?

Fig. 2. Venue checklist.

1. How easy did you find it to locate the venue on your first visit?

2. Is the venue reasonably close to the motorway network or main-line railway station?

3. Will your delegates be driving into a city centre during rush-hour and if so, will the venue still be easy to find?

4. Is there adequate signage already or can you put your own up?

## Assessing the car parking facilities

◆ Does the facility have adequate car parking? If not, where is the nearest public car park?

◆ Is there a car park charge? Do you need to give/ purchase tokens?

◆ Does the hotel have a discount arrangement with the nearest public car park?

◆ Does the car park appear to be safe, i.e. is it manned, is it in an area where cars are likely to be vulnerable to trouble-makers?

## Assessing the suitability of the conference registration area

Ask where the registration desk is usually situated at that particular venue. If the area is not clearly visible to delegates entering the venue, make a note of the fact that adequate signs will be required to point them in the right direction. Ensure that you will have room enough for yourself, staff who may be assisting you, and your delegate packs.

## Assessing the rooms

When considering the suitability of any room, be it a large conference room or a small syndicate room, ensure there is adequate space to be able to accommodate the seating plan you are intending using. The most common types are:

- theatre
- classroom
- boardroom
- U-shaped.

These are illustrated in Figure 3. Ask the advice of the hotel or venue staff, who will be very familiar with each style and what works best in their particular rooms.

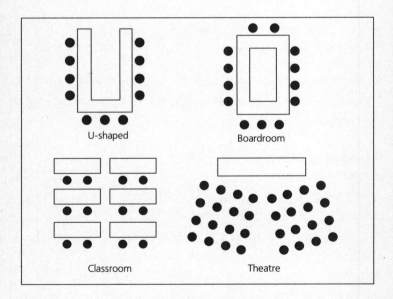

Fig. 3. Seating plans and room styles.

*Working out your needs*

How many rooms are you going to require? This will depend on your programme for the event. You may require just one room set in theatre style, or you may be planning to have the delegates split up into smaller groups for workshops or smaller meetings. If this is the case you will need to have rooms available which are adequate in size, location and content.

In an ideal world the smaller rooms (or breakout/syndicate rooms as they are often called) would be located on the same floor and as close as possible to the main conference room. However, this is often not the case and delegates may have to walk or go by a lift to other floors within the building. If this is the case, are there adequate stairs and/or lifts to be able to cope with the number of people you are expecting? Is there disabled/wheelchair access?

These considerations are important not only in terms of delegate care but to allow you to keep to the schedule. Make a note that adequate signs will be required to ensure delegates don't get lost en route and/or make use of directional staff/stewards.

## Other room considerations

- Be aware that the rooms take time to be set up by the venue staff. It may not be possible to run a 500-delegate conference during the day and then follow it by a formal dinner for 500 in the evening in the same room. Discuss your options with the venue staff.

- Ask about heating/air conditioning – depending on the time of year, you will certainly need either one or the other.

◆ Is there a separate room that can be allocated as a speaker room? This is somewhere for the speakers to have some peace and quiet away from the delegates, maybe to run through their slides to make sure they are in the right order and not upside-down, and generally to collect themselves before their talk.

### The seating arrangements

If you are expecting a large number of delegates, check that all the seating will be as seen, and not topped up with 'cheap seats'. Sitting still all day is hard enough for most people, but sitting still on uncomfortable chairs is close to impossible!

◆ Check whether the seating is cushioned and comfortable or hard and uncomfortable.

### The ceiling height

Some conference facilities, particularly those on lower ground floors, have particularly low ceilings and little or no natural daylight. If you are expecting a large number of delegates you will need to assess whether this will feel too claustrophobic and, if you are planning on using audio visual equipment, whether the ceiling will allow the use of a screen suitable for your needs. Conversely, the room may have such a high ceiling that the acoustics are difficult to work with.

### Assessing the sound

Consider whether microphones will be required in the room and whether there is a sound system already in place.

## Looking at the lighting

The quality of lighting can have a dramatic effect on the event. Ambient lighting is usually favoured, with a spotlight on the speaker. Consider the following:

♦ When the lights go down to darken the room, is your speaker going to disappear too? Will he/she be able to see his/her notes? If not, a lectern light will be needed.

♦ Will the audience be able to see to take notes or refer to other literature?

♦ Where is the control point for the lights situated? In some very modern facilities the control panel is built into the speaker's lectern so they can control the lighting as they see fit; however, by far the most common is a panel at the back of the room.

If you are going to use audio visual equipment you may need to darken the room to a suitable degree. Most modern facilities are able to accommodate blackout, however, some older buildings, such as assembly and state rooms, may have high ornate windows with no blinds or shutters.

## The staging

You may wish to have your speakers seated on a staged area, especially if you are expecting a large audience.

♦ Does the venue have its own staging, either permanently fixed or in movable blocks?

♦ Is there an extra charge for this or is it included in the cost?

## Toilets and cloakroom facilities

No one likes queuing for toilets, especially if they only have 15 minutes in which to get a coffee, stretch their legs and dash to the loo! Adequate bathroom facilities are essential, not only for delegate comfort but to ensure that you will physically be able to keep to your scheduled programme. Queues will be inevitable, but keep them within reason.

◆ Are there adequate disabled facilities?

Particularly in the winter months you may find that delegates wish to leave overcoats and, maybe, overnight bags, etc.

◆ Is a secure cloakroom facility available, and if so it is it staffed and is there a charge for this service?

◆ It may be that a coat rack will be sufficient placed behind the registration desk; is one available for this?

## Fire escapes

Do not take anyone else's word for it, check yourself to see that the fire escapes are clear of clutter and that they do conform to safety requirements.

## Storage facilities

Is there safe and secure storage space for your own and exhibitors' boxes, etc?

## The exhibition space

If you are running an exhibition alongside your conference, or even just displaying information on behalf of the sponsors, ensure that adequate space is available, ideally in the area that will be used for refreshments and not far away from the main conference room. You need to ensure there is room for the actual stands, space for delegates to wander around freely and safely and to establish any Health and Safety regulations which may be enforced by the venue/local authority.

- Are there plenty of electricity sockets?

- Will the exhibitors need a telephone socket? Can this be billed individually by the venue?

- If displaying posters, will suitable display boards be available and what kind of attachment will you need to provide to secure the posters or other graphics to them?

- Are there chairs, tables and table covers available for exhibitors' use?

## Identifying obstructions

Have a good look around the potential conference room and see if there are any obstructions that may create problems if not addressed. The most common are pillars situated in unfortunate places that are sure to block the delegates' view, and low-hung chandeliers that look beautiful but may get in the way of the projection equipment. The problems can usually be resolved, or at least worked around.

## Assessing the facilities available for disabled delegates

- If the conference rooms are not on the ground floor, is

there a suitable sized lift to take anyone using a wheelchair to the appropriate floor?

◆ Are the disabled toilets within a reasonable distance?

◆ If you are expecting delegates who may be hard of hearing, has a deaf-loop system been installed?

## Assessing the catering facilities

The venue should be able to provide you with a selection of sample menus to give you an idea of what they can provide, for what cost.

◆ Take a look at the suggested eating area – if it is a fixed restaurant, is it within a reasonable distance from the conference room?

◆ Will the delegates be taking lunch with other visitors to the venue?

◆ Is the restaurant located in an area where the delegates are likely to wander back to the exhibition area to the awaiting stand-holders, or are they more likely to wander off to somewhere more interesting?

◆ What refreshments are included in the price?

◆ If only morning coffee, lunch and afternoon tea are provided, how much extra will you be required to pay for coffee on arrival?

◆ Do you intend for lunch to be taken seated or standing up?

◆ If seated, will there be room for all of your delegates to eat at one sitting?

- With adequate warning is the venue able to cater for specialised diets, e.g. vegetarians, diabetics, etc?

- Very importantly, do the serving staff look cheerful and are they helpful?

- Is the bar area tidy and well stocked?

**The accommodation**

If you are intending using a hotel facility or any other facility where accommodation is offered and the delegates will be staying overnight, ensure that you also get to view a selection of bedrooms. Consider the following:

- If in a busy city centre are the windows double-glazed?

- What items are available in the rooms?

- Business delegates like to have access to a telephone and many hotels these days also have modem points in the rooms.

- Are tea and coffee-making facilities in the rooms?

- Is a trouser press/iron/hairdryer/skirt hanger provided?

If the venue you are contemplating using does not offer accommodation, the local tourist bureau will be able to help you locate somewhere suitably close to the venue and within your budget. Whilst visiting the venue itself, take time to look at the choice of accommodation available.

## ESTABLISHING WHAT IS INCLUDED

Venues vary enormously as to what is included in the price. Traditional hotel and conference centre venues tend to offer both a **day delegate** rate (sometimes called an 8-hour rate), which could include morning coffee, lunch, afternoon tea and use of the conference room. Venues such as hotels that offer accommodation may be able to offer you a **24-hour delegate** rate which usually includes dinner, bed and breakfast as well as the morning coffee, lunch, afternoon tea and use of the conference room. There is normally room for at least some negotiation on both day and 24-hour delegate rates.

## Ensuring equipment availability

You will need to ascertain whether the price also includes the hire of the lecterns, microphones, spotlights, screens and staging. If not, find out exactly what items are available, what condition they are in, and how much they will cost to hire. If you are going to use an audio visual technician they may prefer to use their own equipment which is likely to be regularly tested and upgraded, rather than the hotel's own possibly outdated and rather temperamental projector.

# 3

# Sourcing Speakers and Setting the Programme

*'It is important to produce an event in which people are interested enough to invest their time, money and energies to attend.'*

## CONDUCTING MARKET RESEARCH

You may be given a brief to produce an event based on a general theme. You will then have to decide on the specific subject areas that are to be included in the programme, and the speakers who are going to present them.

It is important to produce an event in which people are interested enough to invest their time, money and energies to attend. Therefore their opinions matter greatly and some market research can be a worthwhile exercise. To begin your search for subjects a **brainstorming** session with colleagues/superiors can be invaluable. During the session as many different suggestions as possible are called out without discussion and written down for later evaluation. As people bounce ideas off one another, trains of thought can be created and new ideas come to the fore.

## DESIGNING A QUESTIONNAIRE

Having brainstormed possible subjects, put together a

questionnaire asking potential delegates from in-house or external mailing lists to indicate which of the subjects they would be interested in hearing about. You can also ask them to suggest other subjects and speakers who may not already be listed. From the responses you will be able to put together a programme that you can feel confident is going to be attractive to those you want to attend.

**Getting a response**

Do not expect a high response rate, typically 5 per cent will respond, so ensure your circular goes to enough potential delegates to make it worthwhile. You can encourage people to respond by making the questionnaire as short as possible, perhaps only one side of A4, and as easy to complete as possible, e.g. using tick boxes and a simple layout. Enclose a stamped addressed envelope or fax-back option and include an incentive such as a discount on the registration fee to those people who return the questionnaire. As with any correspondence that is sent out, be aware of your corporate image and make it as attractive and inviting as possible.

Always ensure your mailings are permitted within the Data Protection Act. Refer to trade magazines and trade associations to keep up-to-date on the latest news and views in your particular industry to be able to ensure that the programme is topical.

## FINDING SPEAKERS

The importance of good speakers cannot be under-estimated. You may have an excellent venue, a large crowd of delegates and have organised it all perfectly, but if the presentations are poor none of it will have mattered. There are certain characteristics to look for in a potential speaker. They should be:

- knowledgeable about the subject
- articulate
- experienced
- well prepared
- able to empathise with, and enthuse, the audience
- respected.

## Where to find speakers

Your organisation may have contacts with suitable and willing speakers, however, you may be required to look externally for them.

### Call for papers

By notifying appropriate interest groups you may find volunteers who would like to present at the event. The notice can be placed in appropriate journals, sent to university departments, in newsletters, posted on a web site, etc.

The call for papers should include details of the event – date, time, venue – and language of presentation (and whether interpreters will be in attendance) as well as organisers' details. Guidelines should be included as to how to apply. It is usual to ask for a written abstract of a specified number of words which outlines the presentation, as well as a biography of the speaker.

You will find that you will not be short of volunteers. Many companies may find that this opportunity would suit their marketing objectives very well indeed and will be prepared to cover all speaker expenses. If you get more abstracts offered than you need you may be able to hold on to them for future events. (See Figure 4.)

### Other events

By attending other similar/competing events, you will be able to identify for yourself which speakers perform well and which don't. Consider how they are received by the audience and in any press reports after the event. Like celebrities, it is possible for speakers to be over-exposed. Popular and prolific speakers are fine so long as their material remains fresh and they do not become complacent. You may also need to book popular speakers some months in advance to ensure their availability.

### Speaker bureaux

Speaker bureaux are agencies of, sometimes professional, speakers. A good bureau can be an enormous help in finding the right speaker for your event, but obviously at a price. Some agencies specialise in particular fields and their staff are knowledgeable about the subject matter. Look for a member of the IGAB – International Group of Agencies and Bureaux – so that you can be sure the agency abides by a strict code of practice. They can also provide celebrities for after-dinner speeches, opening ceremonies, etc.

### Members of Parliament

Government Ministers and other Members of Parliament are frequently asked to talk at conferences, often in the role of keynote speaker at the start of the event. This can be very worthwhile, particularly in terms of media

---

**Press Release**
**SECURITY FOCUS '0X**
**UK Security Association Announce 'Call for Papers'**

In preparation for the 200X International Security Focus Conference the UK Security Association would be pleased to receive papers for selection at this important event. The conference, in October 200X at the National Training Centre in Oxfordshire, will consist of a number of individual sessions each comprising three 35-minute presentations focusing on issues that provide information on the latest trends and issues facing the security industry. Depending on the nature of each session, the attendees will consist of end users, specifiers, manufacturers, etc from the UK and overseas, as well as industry-related personnel, including representatives from many police forces, government bodies, etc.

Submissions are welcome from the UK and overseas and should take the following form:

◆ In the first instance an abstract of approx. 500 words should be submitted in English by 15th May 200X for consideration by an industry panel. Early submissions are encouraged.

◆ Although submissions from commercial companies are very much encouraged, the paper should not be regarded as an advertisement for that company. There will be a number of complementary advertising opportunities during the conference but the content of the presentation should not include direct references to a company's products unless used to illustrate a point.

◆ Papers should be accompanied by a brief career biography of the proposed presenter, including experience of presenting.

◆ On acceptance the speaker will be required to send a full copy of their paper up to 10 sides (5 A4 pages) in length as well as on disk or via email.

◆ For any queries regarding this 'call for papers', please contact Polly Marston at the UK Security Association events office on 01200 789123.

Please send submissions to: Polly Marston, UK Security Association.....

Fig. 4. Call for papers.

attraction. As their official diaries tend to be booked well in advance you may need much longer notice of the event than with other speakers. The MPs will often stay only for a short while and will be accompanied by their secretary or assistant and possibly other officials. You will be expected to correspond in detail with the Minister's office to make the necessary arrangements, which may include security and other matters. Also be prepared to be let down at short notice should parliamentary business prevent them attending. It is worthwhile having a contingency plan in place.

## CORRESPONDING WITH SPEAKERS

Having chosen your speakers, keep them informed and updated on progress as the conference gets closer. Send them a letter thanking them for agreeing to speak, and making clear the terms of the booking. For example, you may or may not be paying a speaker fee or honorarium, travelling expenses, etc. If this is clear from the start there should be no room for misunderstandings later on. (See Figure 5.)

### Speaker rehearsals

In an ideal world all of the conference speakers would attend a rehearsal in advance of the event to ensure that their presentation skills are satisfactory, that their papers do not overlap in terms of content, that their presentations fill the time schedule correctly and that they are familiar with the venue and audio visual facilities. In reality the first time you meet the speakers may be on the day of the event, half an hour before the start of the presentation. Speakers are often very busy people and,

Mr David Church
Area Training Dept
Dental Association of Great Britain
1 Allsorts Gardens
London
SW5

29th October 200X

Dear David,

Ref: Dental Technicians Conference, March 200X

Further to our conversation this morning, I would like formally to invite you to present a paper at the Dental Technicians Conference to be held at the Amblay Manor Hotel and Conference Centre, Wychbold, on 15th March 200X.

The conference is an annual event, this year consisting of six papers of 40 minutes duration each. At the end of the conference there will be a question and answer session to the panel of four speakers. This year's chosen theme is **Training and Careers in the Dental Industry** and I know that you are well placed to speak on the subject of **Training in the New Millennium**.

I would like to confirm that we shall be able to pay you a speaker honorarium of £100 plus travelling expenses at 35p per mile or standard class rail fare.

I will forward a speaker information pack to you in the next week which will contain further details of the event. In the meantime if you have any queries please do not hesitate to contact me.

Yours sincerely,

Fig. 5. Invitation to speaker.

particularly if not being paid for the exercise, may not be inclined to find extra time to travel to the venue or other location to rehearse – in which case, alternatives need to be sought.

### Presentation skills

If the speaker is an unknown quantity and you are in any doubt as to the quality of the presentation skills of the speaker, you could travel to meet them and have them do a short presentation for you. Alternatively video footage or anecdotal evidence from experienced and known conference delegates/organisers may help to allay your fears.

### Time allocation

Ask the speakers to time themselves rehearsing their presentation and be clear as to whether their time allocation includes questions from the audience, or whether that will be in addition.

### Overlap

Overlap can be minimised by providing very clear briefs and issuing a copy of each of the abstracts (or scripts) to each of the speakers, particularly those who are speaking on a similar subject. This, of course, is subject to you being supplied with the abstracts; when requesting them in the speaker pack emphasis should be put on the fact that it really is essential, and will be required at least two weeks (if not longer) in advance of the event. This will allow time for rewriting if necessary. Provide contact details for fellow speakers so that they can discuss presentations if required.

*Overseas speakers*

You may have an increased chance of speakers arriving for rehearsals if they have flown in from overseas, particularly if they have had a long-haul flight. You should allow for jet-lag when making the flight arrangements and give them adequate time to re-orientate themselves.

*Set-up day*

It may be possible to set up your conference on the day prior to the event. This will probably result in an additional charge by the venue but this is normally at a reduced rate and is very worthwhile in terms of peace of mind. A good night's sleep is more likely to be had if you have already tested the audio visual equipment, erected the signs, prepared the registration area and set up display stands, etc.

## Speaker information packs

A pack of information pertinent to the speaker and chairperson will be useful, and could include the following:

*Background information on your organisation*

They may be unfamiliar with the aims and objectives of your organisation and this will help them to understand 'where you are coming from'.

*Overview of event*

The aims and objectives of the event and a very brief history if it has run before.

*Details of presentation required*
A clear brief as to the presentation you are asking them to create and deliver, as well as the duration and timing of it.

*Details of the event*
Date, time, venue.

*Summary of the target audience*
The speaker will then be able to adapt his/her talk to suit the understanding of those delegates.

*Presentation details of other speakers*
Subjects to be covered by other speakers in your session, and possibly contact telephone numbers.

*Details of session chairperson*
Including contact details if appropriate.

*Written requirements*
What is required from them in terms of a biography, abstract, etc, and when. It is important that you receive this information well in advance of the event in order for you to be able to distribute it to the chairperson, publish details in the programme, etc. Set a date according to your schedule and then move it forward by a week to allow for late responses.

*Audio visual requirements form*
It is vital to establish what is required well in advance of the event. Emphasise that they should not presume equipment will be available if they have not informed you of its need.

*Clear directions/map*
Easy to read and accurate.

*Details of what to do on arrival*
Make it as easy as possible for speakers on the day of the event by giving them details of where to go and what to do on arrival.

*Details of lunch/hotel accommodation*
Include a note for speakers to inform you if any special dietary requirements are necessary, e.g. vegetarians, allergies, etc.

Include directions to the hotel if different to the venue and make it clear what is being provided, such as 'We will provide bed and breakfast in the Highclere Hotel. Please note that you will be responsible for any other expenses in relation to your stay.'

*Parking pass*
If applicable.

*Useful hints and tips*
A few guidelines on how to make the most of their presentation. Even experienced speakers could do with reminding sometimes. See Figure 6.

*Details of sponsors*
If appropriate.

*How and when to claim expenses*
If applicable.

---

## SUGGESTIONS FOR SPEAKERS

◆ Keep text to a minimum on visual aids.

◆ Do not blatantly plug your company during your talk. This can have the negative effect of alienating the audience. Your very presence and the high quality of your talk will be an excellent advertisement for your company.

◆ Make eye contact with the audience as often as possible.

◆ Do not read from a script, use prompt cards instead.

◆ Rehearse your presentation and ensure it is designed to fit the time allocated. It would be a great shame if the chairperson informed you that you have only two minutes left when you haven't yet reached the main crux of the presentation.

◆ Ensure you arrive in plenty of time to prepare your visual aids and generally to orientate yourself before your talk.

◆ Detailed advice for both novice and professional speakers can be found in *Mastering Public Speaking* (How To Books).

---

Fig. 6. Speaker hints and tips.

*Contact details for queries*
Details of how and when speakers can reach you, including on-site.

*A feedback form*
Opinion as to the success of the event is important from the speaker's point of view as well as the delegates, so give them an opportunity to be constructively critical.

*A checklist for speakers*
So that they can easily see when they need to return the various forms, and check themselves to see if they have done so.

## UNDERSTANDING THE ROLE OF THE CHAIRPERSON

The **chairperson's** (or moderator's) role is principally to introduce each speaker to the audience, to ensure they do not overrun their allotted time and to provide the link between each talk. They could also summarise at the end of each talk and field questions from the audience to the speaker or panel of speakers. The chairperson also reads out housekeeping notices such as evacuation details in case of an emergency, order of presentation if changed from the published programme and messages from the organisers. An experienced chairperson who can 'work' an audience is worth his/her weight in gold. Often the job will go to an official from a major sponsor or someone from the organising committee.

# (4)

# The Conference Brochure

*'The brochure is the sales document of the conference.'*

## DESIGNING THE BROCHURE

The conference brochure should appeal to those potential delegates you have identified, set the tone for the event and provide standard information.

Ask yourself a few questions before you start:

- Who is the conference aimed at?

- What information does the brochure need to contain?

- What feedback will you need?

- Are there certain commitments you have made to the sponsors regarding the inclusion and positioning of their logos?

- How will the brochures be circulated?

- How do other organisations design their conference brochures?

Be sure of who you are targeting. Use language the recipients will be familiar with and avoid the use of unnecessary or irrelevant jargon.

## What information should it contain/what feedback will you require?

The brochure will need to contain all necessary information for the delegate, as well as the return booking form containing the information that you will require to process the booking.

| *Information delegates need* | *Information you need* |
|---|---|
| title of conference | name of delegate |
| description | company |
| location | position |
| date | mailing address |
| time | postcode |
| speakers | phone number |
| subjects | fax number |
| price and method of payment | email address |
| what's included in price | invoice address if different |
| how to book | purchase order number |
| closing date for applications | person to be invoiced |
| sponsors' details | credit card details if |
| VAT number | applicable |
| payment method for overseas delegates | demographics – to be completed |
| phone number for enquiries | sessions of choice |
| cancellation policy. | special dietary requirements. |

### Useful tips

Also remember to:

◆ Make sure it is faxable, i.e. not too much black/dark space or shading.

- Provide a downloadable PDF version.

- Leave lots of white space – don't make it look too crowded or over-complicated.

- Make it easy to read and understand.

- Edit, re-edit and edit again.

- Make it attractive to look at.

- Make it look professional even if on a tight budget – remember it is your first contact with the delegate and it must impress.

- Make it as simple as possible.

- Even for non-paying events, it is useful to have a form returned so that you can establish how many delegates you will need to cater for.

- Ensure essential information that needs to be retained by the delegates is not placed on the reverse side of the registration form. Further details can be found in Appendix 4.

- Ensure it complies with the Data Protection Act.

**Choosing who designs it**

These days many people are conversant with desktop publishing and are capable of designing their own brochures, a task simplified by dedicated software such as Microsoft Publisher. Ideas can be 'borrowed' from other brochures. Keep a file of any you come across so that you can decide for yourself what works and what doesn't. Alternatively you may consider using a design agency. You will find design agencies listed in local telephone directories, or your local printer may offer this service themselves or may be able to put you in contact with a suitable agency. Obtain several quotes before placing your business as prices will vary considerably. When briefing the agency, ensure your wishes are clear and proof-read the final copy before printing.

## PRINTING THE BROCHURE

The look and the feel of the conference brochure will make a big statement about the conference. A shabbily put together document with spelling mistakes and poor grammar will not suggest that the conference will be a well managed, well produced event that your delegates should spend their time and money attending. Conversely, a well designed, glossy brochure that is clear and concise will put the potential delegate in a positive frame of mind.

### Choosing the paper

Choose the paper carefully. If you are working on a tight budget you may not be able to afford glossy paper, but you could make good use of colour. Pastel shades are easy on the eye and will also fax clearly, conversely a deep colour will often be illegible after faxing.

Use at least 100gsm paper – it needs to be resilient and withstand being photocopied, filed, mailed and returned. If you are incorporating a reply-paid coupon then the Post Office requires the thickness to be no less that 235 microns and A6 minimum in size.

Proof-read time and time again. And when you are sure everything is correct, do it again. Also ask at least one other person to go over it as you may find that you have become 'blind' to mistakes if you have been working on the document for too long.

### Costing the printing

As with design agencies, the cost of printing will vary from company to company and from paper type to paper type, so obtain a selection of quotes. Generally the first print run will include the preparation of the plates used in the printing process, and the cost difference per thousand after that will not be huge. It will be helpful to let the printer know in advance when to expect the camera ready copy, and the date by which the finished documents will be needed. This will enable the printer to build it into the print schedule. If possible give printers a deadline which is earlier than necessary to allow for unforeseen circumstances. Also bear in mind that print runs required at short notice will often cost more. An absolute minimum of one week will be required.

Digital printing is much more flexible. Ask your printer for advice on your particular project.

### DISTRIBUTING THE BROCHURE

Having given much thought to the content and design of the brochure, you now need to get it in front of your potential delegates. Who they are will determine how you reach them.

### Mailing options
◆ in-house mailing lists
◆ membership lists
◆ previous delegates

- purchasing lists from mailing companies
- magazine inserts
- 'piggy back' mailings with companies you may have connections with who are targeting similar individuals
- lists obtained from publications, directories, registers and the local Chamber of Commerce.

If you can send the brochure to a named individual rather than 'Marketing Manager, XYZ Products Ltd' for example, it will be much more likely to reach them.

Whether using in-house or bought-in mailing lists, ensure they are 'clean', i.e. names are not duplicated. As well as being uneconomical, in our world of constant unsolicited junk mail people have low tolerance thresholds.

*Electronic distribution*
If your organisation has a website, put the programme and booking details on it.

*Postage*
If doing a very large mailing, professional mailing houses will fill the envelopes, frank and dispatch them for a fee, and a reduction can sometimes be gained in the mailing cost. Ask your Post Office about Mailsort and and other bulk mailing options or check the Royal Mail website www.royalmail.com > BulkMailSavings.

# 5

# Working to a Schedule

*'A well structured approach to the task of organising your conference is essential and will bring many benefits.'*

## SCHEDULING THE EVENT

Twelve weeks can normally be considered an adequate lead-time for events. This allows satisfactory time for preparation, and for press releases to be received and published in the relevant monthly journals. Prior to the 12-week countdown to the event you will have:

- set the budget
- researched and booked the venue
- decided on the content of your programme and copy for the brochure
- booked the speakers
- and be ready to mail out the printed programmes.

### When to send the brochure

Events, organisations and budgets will combine to dictate what is and what is not possible. Presuming the initial mailshot is sent 12 weeks in advance of the event it could be followed by a written or telephone reminder to those who have not yet booked at eight weeks, and then again four weeks out.

Although requiring longer notice of events, there is a tendency for delegates to book their place as late as possible, especially if purchase orders have to be passed through accounting departments. Although to be expected, this can be frustrating for the organiser who needs to be able to anticipate delegate attendance numbers as early as possible. It can be useful to offer an 'early bird' price to encourage early bookings. The resulting increase in early registrations will provide an indication of how the event is being received by potential delegates. This can be useful to help you plan and implement your promotional activity.

*Finding other targets*
By analysing delegate details as they book you can target other potential delegates. For instance, if you find that the conference is attracting a large number of people in a particular job function, or in similar demographic groups, you could direct-mail other people in similar positions.

## CREATING A PLAN
Time is a valuable resource of which few of us seem to have enough. Once time has passed it cannot be replaced, so use it wisely. Whether it is your free time or your work time it is difficult to place an exact figure on the cost of you performing a given task.

### Benefits of using a time plan
◆ You will be able to identify tasks and allocate staff/resources/your own time as required to deal with them.

◆ You will be able to organise your normal work-load around the event and the organisation.

◆ By their very nature some tasks must be done at the last minute, e.g. preparation of badges and stuffing delegate packs. Others need to be carried out some time in advance, such as finding sponsors and distributing programmes. A visual plan will help you to put the pieces together in the correct order and fill any gaps with tasks that, within reason, have no time requirements, like choosing menus. See Figures 7 and 8, which indicate key elements that must be addressed and can be used as a basis for your own plan.

## SCHEDULING THE PROGRAMME

Your brief will dictate the duration of the event – a day, evening or two days perhaps. The programme has to fill that space adequately, ensuring delegates have time to absorb what they're hearing, but not get bored. Remember that we all have relatively short concentration spans, so shorter bursts of information interspersed with lighter input are most likely to be retained.

### Timing it right

*The right time to start*

Consider how the majority of delegates are likely to travel to the venue. By car? By train? By tube? Avoiding the necessity for travel in peak times if at all possible will help ensure delegates arrive in a good frame of mind.

*Refreshment breaks*

Ensure adequate time is built into the programme for the number of anticipated delegates to get themselves a drink and go to the toilet during the refreshment breaks. Similarly at lunchtime the delegates will need to get to the

| Wk bg. | | | | | |
|---|---|---|---|---|---|
| **Before or during Wk 12** | **Wk 11** | **Wk 10** | **Wk 9** | **Wk 8** | **Wk 7** |
| Design/print/distribute programme | | | Receive sponsors' payments | Establish exhibitor requirements | |
| Confirm venue/speakers/sponsors (& invoice sponsors) | Send speaker packs | Design & load website | AV form returns start | | AV forms returned |
| Block-book hotel | Set up registration system | | Order sponsored items, e.g. bags | | |
| Book/confirm contractors | | Send sponsor & exhibitor info. packs | | | |
| Advance press notice & monthly mags | Design/seek approval of layout of sponsored items | | Press release 1 | | |

| Wk 6 | Wk 5 | Wk 4 | Wk 3 | Wk 2 | Event Week |
|---|---|---|---|---|---|
| Confirm menus | Print bags | Photocopy speaker papers etc | Take delivery of delegate pack inserts | Closing date for applications | Everything not done between wk 12 & now! |
| Confirm AV requirements to contractor | Hotel room allocation | Revisit venue & conduct risk assessment | Take delivery of sponsored items, e.g. pens etc. | Prepare delegate packs | |
| | Press release 2 | | Provide approx. catering nos. | Press release 3 | |
| | Invoice sponsors | | Circulate rehearsal schedule | Confirm final numbers to venue | |
| | Print catalogue or programme | | | Confirm final rooming list | |

Post event: analyse evaluation forms, finalise budget and debrief. Ongoing throughout 12-week countdown: handle registration/enquiries.

Fig. 7. Time plan illustration (i).

This planner is less detailed and monitors only key tasks. It could be used in conjunction with a more detailed planner.

| Task | Target Date | Completion Date | Actioned by |
|---|---|---|---|
| Identify brief | | | |
| Budget projection | | | |
| Budget actual | | | |
| Venue visits | | | |
| Venue confirmation | | | |
| Speaker programme confirmed | | | |
| Brochure design/print | | | |
| Brochures mailed | | | |
| PR activity Pre-event 1, 2 & 3 Post-event | | | |
| Accommodation booked | | | |
| Delegate pack items received & packed | | | |
| AV requirements confirmed | | | |
| De-brief | | | |

Fig. 8. Time plan illustration (ii).

lunch room, consume their lunch, network, stretch their legs and get some fresh air, and go to the toilet. The number and location of toilets available at the venue of your choice, the location of the lunch room, the presence of exhibitors and the number of delegates will have a direct bearing on these timings.

*Location of conference rooms*
If the conference is spread throughout a number of rooms, ensure that enough time is built into the

APBC Autumn Seminar

## A Closer Look at Ethology
*(Including half-day workshops on cats, horses and rabbits)*

| | |
|---|---|
| 09.30 – 10.00 | Registration and coffee |
| 10.00 – 10.05 | Welcome<br>David Appleby Dip CABC |
| 10.05 – 10.50 | Evolutionary constraints on species specific behaviour in the cat<br>John Bradshaw PhD |
| 10.50 – 11.15 | Coffee break |
| 11.15 – 12.05 | Problem horses? Problem owners?<br>Understanding equine behavioural strategies<br>Cecilia Lindberg BA, MA, PhD |
| 12.05 – 12.50 | Behaviour modification – working with natural behaviours<br>Emma Magnus BSc(Hons) MSc |
| 12.50 – 14.00 | Buffet lunch |
| 14.00 – 15.15 | Workshops |

**1: Understanding and reducing stress in cats – a practical approach**
Sarah Heath BVSc MRCVS and Sandra McCune VN BA(Mod) PhD

**2: The Natural Horse**
Neil Davidson BSc(Hons) and Natalie Waran PhD

**3: Benjamin Bunny or Roger Rabbit? Rabbit behaviour problems – prevention and modification.**
Anne McBride BSc, PhD, Cert Cons, FRSA and Christine Huggett BSc(Hons) PhD

| | |
|---|---|
| 15.15 – 15.45 | Coffee |
| 15.45 – 16.30 | Workshops as above |
| 16.30 | Depart |

Fig. 9. Conference programme.

programme for the delegates to be able to move from one to another. This is particularly important if the rooms are on different floors. It is very distracting and most unfair to speakers to have delegates wandering into their presentations late. Consider how the delegates will move from one room to another. Do they need to use a lift? If so, how many lifts are there? Where are they situated? How many 'lift-loads' of delegates are going to be moving? Do not base this judgement on the time it takes you and the venue co-ordinator to walk the same route during your recce. Delegates will walk slower, will probably be chatting and not necessarily paying attention to signs, or they may get distracted by something more interesting along the way. Even if the rooms are located on the same floor and close together still expect some delay. Delegates will use the opportunity to nip to the toilets, make phone calls and to get some fresh air.

*The graveyard slot*
After lunch everyone undergoes a lull whilst our bodies are busy digesting food. The resulting dip in energy levels means that whilst the speaker is getting high on nerve-induced adrenalin the delegates are resisting the urge (hopefully) to fall asleep, hence the term 'graveyard slot'. To help keep everyone on their toes, make sure the room is not too warm and schedule a lively and entertaining speaker with a particularly interesting subject.

*Consecutive days*
If running at two-day event, delegates may not need to register on the second day. It is wise not to start too early in the morning if the schedule allows, as you may find

delegates wander in late. Alternatively put a very interesting paper that no one wants to miss on first.

The date of your event may be dictated to you, giving you no control over it. Alternatively you may have some freedom to decide on the best date.

*Weekend or weekday?*
Weekend rates are usually substantially cheaper, however choosing a weekend may not be suitable for a business event and don't forget many venues get booked up with weddings well in advance, often on Saturdays from May through to October.

*Holiday time or competing events?*
Consider the time of year. Are there any other major events being held which would draw your delegates away? Is it a peak holiday time? Too soon before/after Christmas? This can be of particular importance if delegates will be paying their own fees and expenses rather than companies.

# 6

# Setting up a Registration System

*'It is important that the registration system which you decide upon is as simple as possible.'*

## USING COMPUTERISED REGISTRATION SYSTEMS

There are an increasing number of software packages available to conference organisers that can streamline the whole registration process. By entering the delegate details just once you can automatically produce:

♦ a personalised letter of confirmation
♦ a badge
♦ an invoice
♦ and allocate workshops, hotel bookings, etc.

Windows® formatted modules can be incorporated to plan and track accommodation, catering, partner programmes, excursions, budgets, etc and may also include a register of venues. Each of the growing number of software packages have different benefits and considerations so it is worth seeing a demonstration of each, and if possible talking to current users of the systems. Most can be networked so that a number of people can access and use the system. Some can be purchased in modules allowing you to pay for only those modules that will be of use to you. As is standard with most computer software packages, technical support is available for registered users.

## Assessing costs

Always look carefully at the cost and terms of the support offered, which although probably essential can, in some cases, be quite prohibitive. However, the time that these software packages can save in administration and reporting can be very substantial.

## Modifying your existing software

If you are organising your first conference for a society or association you may well not have the luxury of a dedicated software program. In this case one alternative is to have your own program written by a computer programmer. It can be designed to suit your exact requirements and hardware but will still incur possibly high costs in programmers' fees. If considering your own custom-made program remember that technical support may still be needed on an on-going basis, and check that the programmer will be able to provide this.

## WEB-BASED REGISTRATION SYSTEMS

Web-based registration systems are becoming increasingly popular and look very professional, with some organisers using these as their preferred or only booking facility. Using a pre-set format delegates are able to book online and make payments, receive automated confirmation details, etc. You can purchase specialist software or use a service provider. Most systems are very flexible, and you may only need to purchase or hire specific modules.

## OTHER REGISTRATION OPTIONS

### Data companies

Some organisations choose to delegate the registration process to a specialist registration company. These companies are experienced in handling registrations for all kinds of conferences and exhibitions, and can provide other associated services such as invoicing, credit control, badging, mailings, etc. The companies can provide staff and the equipment for computerised on-site registration as well as handling pre-event registrations. It is worth discussing your requirements with one or two registration companies to establish exactly what they can do for you, and at what cost.

Find out what they can offer that you cannot, or most likely do not, have time to do yourself. The cost of professional registration services may prove prohibitive for the smaller conference but with larger events are worth giving some consideration to. As with all event professionals, do not think of the cost alone. Consider the other, less tangible, benefits of having experienced personnel with a computerised and efficient system in the front line.

### Dealing with registration in-house

You may decide to handle the bookings and enquiries yourself, or at least keep it in-house. This need not be the daunting task it may appear, so long as a system is put into place to ensure that it is as automated as possible. Decide on your system before the first bookings arrive.

## SETTING UP YOUR OWN IN-HOUSE MANUAL SYSTEM

All delegates registering to attend the event, whether fee-paying or otherwise, will require a confirmation that their booking has been received and they are expected to attend. The confirmation document can include a number of items such as directions, instructions for when they arrive, reminder of the registration time, etc. Ensure the letter, in keeping with the brochure and any other literature issued, is attractive, unambiguous and follows the house-style if appropriate.

### What to include in the information pack

*Directions*
The venue should be able to provide you with a map to issue to all attendees. Make sure that it is up-to-date. It is not uncommon for new roundabouts and traffic systems to be put in place whilst the venue merrily carries on issuing the same map, causing unnecessary grief to the delegates in the process.

There are companies who will provide maps of any given area customised to your own specification. These look very attractive and can incorporate your own logos. (Perhaps yet another sponsorship opportunity?)

*Invoice/receipt*
You will have already established whether or not payment is to be made at the time of booking or whether individuals can be invoiced. This is a decision that should be made in conjunction with the organisation's accounting department or honorary treasurer.

Similarly credit card payments will need to be processed according to the organisation's normal practice. The registration process can get very complicated if the payments have to be separated and sent to the accounts department for processing, and the protracted process can also increase the room for error and mislaid documents. You will have to discuss the implications of this with appropriate management and find a system that will work for you all.

### Confirmation details

The letter of confirmation should be, as usual, in line with the company/organisation's corporate image, and should be welcoming and clear. Instructions should be precise and unambiguous. Remind delegates of the registration time and whether coffee will be available to them on arrival. (See Figure 10.)

### Badges

Some organisers dispatch badges with the letter of confirmation to save time and prevent unnecessary queuing during the registration period. If this is the case they should be instructed to bring the badge with them to gain entry and to collect a badge holder (if used) when they register.

Make a note of all correspondence with delegates so that you know exactly what has been dispatched and when. Should any delegates have any queries you will then be able to check the dispatch details immediately. Keeping a file of the completed and processed booking forms, in alphabetical order to be taken on site, will ensure that you will quickly be able to look up any particular delegate's queries.

Please reply to:
Pauline Appleby, Conference Manager
Interface Event Management Ltd
Upper Street, Defford, Worcs
WR8 9AB. Tel: 01386 750534
Fax: 01386 750743
www.interfaceconferences.co.uk

Mr T. Morgan
IT Dept
Woodchester University
University Road
Woodchester
WD1 2BC

Dear Mr Trevor Morgan

### Virtual World Conference – Wednesday 12th June 200X

Thank you for registering to attend the Virtual World Conference at the Multi Media Centre, University of Woodlow. I have pleasure in enclosing your receipt and a map/directions for your convenience. The University lies to the west of the Uplands–Barlow section of the A985 (Barlow Road) and to the south-west of the A85 (Markets Road), about 6 miles south of Worcester, and $1^{1}/_{4}$ miles north of Malvern. The Multi Media Centre is accessed from the **Central Campus entrance.**

### Travel & useful numbers
By train: Nearest station – Malvern (hourly service from London Paddington – journey time 2 hrs). Full timetable details can be obtained by calling 0345 484950.
National Express coaches: 0990 808080.
By road: Approx, journey time from London 2 hrs, Oxford 1 hr. Birmingham 40 mins.
By air: Birmingham International Airport 0121 767 5511.
Taxi: Jim's Taxis 01684 555555.

We look forward to welcoming you for coffee and registration between 8am and 9.15am on Wednesday 12th June.

If you have any queries regarding your booking please do not hesitate to contact me on 01386 750534.

With kind regards,
Yours sincerely


Pauline Appleby
Conference Manager

Fig. 10. Delegate confirmation letter.

*Notification of workshop allocation*
If workshop places have been designated, relevant details such as time and location could be included in the letter of confirmation.

*A list of useful numbers and travel hints*
Supply the name and telephone number of a local taxi firm, rail enquiry number, nearest airport, etc. Also indicate the most convenient tube station if the event is in London. By contacting London Transport you may be able to obtain tube maps and other helpful leaflets that you can include in the information pack.

## REGISTERING DELEGATES ON-SITE

It is important that the registration system which you decide upon is as simple as possible. Before the arrival of computerised registration systems it was usual for badges to be laid out in alphabetical order on the registration desk. This is derided these days by some professional organisers, but although not terribly sophisticated it is a reliable and effective method of registering delegates. The badges are easy to locate as each individual arrives at the desk, and it is easy to see at a glance who is and who is not in attendance. For security reasons an alternative method is to put the badges in alphabetical order in a long box so that unregistered delegates are unable to 'assume' the identity of someone who is pre-registered. If packs, papers, bags, etc are also to be handed out ensure they are laid out in an obvious order. If space allows you could have separate tables so that delegates can register and collect their badge at one table and then move on to a second table to collect their packs, etc. This also encourages delegates to move away from the main area of registration as quickly as possible.

Keep an area free for dealing with late payments and queries, and ensure that you have all the items to hand that you may need, such as receipts, pens and credit card facilities. Remember to book a phone line if an automated credit card facility is to be used.

# 7

# Planning Budgets and Sponsorship

*'Before even starting to think about venues, location, speakers, etc the budget must be established.'*

## SETTING BUDGETS

The budget is a quantitative goal which states the financial confines in which you are working. It is the target against which costings (the actual price you will be paying) will be measured. The budget may be given to you as part of your brief, or it may be up to you to prepare your own budget and to justify the costs to your superiors. If a substantial amount of the costs are to be met by sponsorship, you will need to prepare a plan as to how you are going to achieve it. All of this needs to take place before you start your event countdown.

### Looking at the costs

Although the budget should be set at the start of the project it can be altered and monitored as you proceed. The combined costs must fall within your budget figures.

*Fixed costs*

**Fixed costs** are those costs that will be encountered irrespective of the number of delegates who may attend. For example:

- brochure printing
- brochure design
- organisation fees
- speaker fees
- travel
- accommodation
- room hire
- press and publicity
- advertising
- mailing house
- signs.

### Variable costs
**Variable costs** are those which vary according to the number of delegates who attend, e.g. catering costs.

### Income
Income may come from different sources and can also be categorised as **fixed** and **variable**.

### Fixed income
Income that is not dependent on the number of delegates. For example:

- sponsorship
- contribution from organisation.

### Variable income
Income that is not fixed. It may for example vary according to the number of delegates purchasing tickets and the number of exhibitors booking stands.

**NW Regional Conference – Budget**

|  |  | Income | Expenditure | Total |  |
|---|---|---|---|---|---|
| **Fixed costs** |  |  |  |  |  |
|  | Venue hire |  | 175.00 |  |  |
|  | Print brochure |  | 750.00 |  |  |
|  | Speaker fees |  | 350.00 |  |  |
|  | Mailing |  | 300.00 |  |  |
|  | Advertising/PR |  | 250.00 |  |  |
|  | AV hire |  | 300.00 | 2125.00 |  |
| **Variable costs** |  |  |  |  |  |
|  | Buffet/refreshments £15 x 150 |  | 2250.00 |  |  |
|  |  |  |  | 4375.00 |  |
|  | Exhibitors @ £250.00 |  |  |  |  |
|  | 5 | 1250 | Profit | (3125.00) |  |
|  | 10 | 2500 |  | (1875.00) |  |
|  | 15 | 3750 |  | ( 625.00) |  |

This example budget is for a non-profit making conference and assumes that the design of brochure and supply of staff has been handled in-house. This could also be itemised if necessary to identify the true cost of the event. Bracketed figures indicate negative amounts.

Fig. 11. Example budget – projected.

**NW Regional Conference – Budget**

|  |  | Income | Expenditure | Total | Actual | Actual total |
|---|---|---|---|---|---|---|
| **Fixed costs** |  |  |  |  |  |  |
|  | Venue hire |  | 175.00 |  | 175.00 |  |
|  | Print brochure |  | 750.00 |  | 725.00 |  |
|  | Speaker fees |  | 350.00 |  | 350.00 |  |
|  | Mailing |  | 300.00 |  | 287.00 |  |
|  | Advertising/PR |  | 250.00 |  | 207.00 |  |
|  | AV hire |  | 300.00 | 2125.00 | 320.00 | 2064.00 |
| **Variable costs** |  |  |  |  |  |  |
|  | Buffet/ refreshments £15 x 150 |  | 2250.00 |  | 2070.00 |  |
|  |  |  |  | 4375.00 |  | 4134.00 |
|  | Exhibitors @ £250.00 |  |  |  |  |  |
|  | 5 | 1250 | Profit | (3125.00) |  |  |
|  | 10 | 2500 |  | (1875.00) | 1875.00 | (2259.00) |
|  | 15 |  | 3750 | ( 625.00) |  |  |

The actual figures indicate that the conference has cost £2259.00 to produce.

Fig. 12. Example budget – actual.

## Value Added Tax

Value Added Tax (VAT) will be added to many costs of goods and services supplied and will be added to the ticket price if your organisation is registered for VAT. For the purpose of the budget the VAT should not be included on any of the entries so that a true figure is seen. The exception to this rule is if the organising company or organisation is not VAT registered, in which case they will not charge VAT on the ticket sales and will be unable to reclaim VAT on expenditure so the entire cost will need to be met. To find the VAT content in a cost, divide the cost by 47, then multiply by 7. For example, £10.00 ÷ 47 × 7 = £1.49 (rounded up) (so long as VAT remains at 17.5%).

## Breaking even

A **break-even point** is the point at which the conference makes enough income to cover the fixed costs. If the conference is income-generating it is important to know what this figure is so that you have a quantifiable goal to aim for. To find the break-even point, see Figure 13. Further details on practical budgeting can be found in *Managing Budgets and Cash Flows* (How To Books).

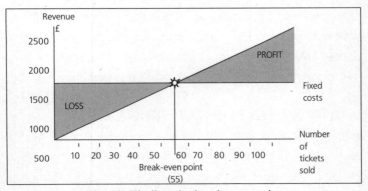

Fig. 13. Finding the break-even point.
We can see that 55 tickets need to be sold to break even to meet the fixed costs of £1,750.

## INSURING AGAINST DISASTERS

The thorny issue of insurance should be addressed and a management decision made as to whether or not to take up one of the specialised insurance policies that are available. No matter how hard we try, some things really are beyond our control, such as the weather, rail strikes, terrorist activity, etc. In instances where conferences are drastically affected by these things, adequate and appropriate insurance can make the difference between an inconvenience and a financial disaster. Policies can be taken out to reimburse organisers for a range of mishaps, including:

- cancellation/abandonment
- non-appearance of speakers
- reduced attendance by delegates
- failure to vacate the venue by the specified time
- legal liabilities
- personal accident and travel.

### Checking your cover

Check your organisation's own insurance policy and establish the situation regarding the venue's insurance policy. The items left uncovered by either of these are what you now need to look at. There are several specialist insurance companies who can provide flexible packages, so discuss your situation and obtain quotes from them. You may be surprised at how reasonable the premium can be.

## CONTROLLING THE CATERING COSTS

Every venue you visit will be able to supply you with an assortment of menus that can be provided in a range of budgets. You may be offered a day delegate rate which includes lunch and refreshments or you may be offered a room hire rate with catering costs separate. This is often the case with civic and more unusual buildings, where the facility is leased to a catering company and all payments relating to catering costs are made directly to them. If offered a day delegate rate check exactly what it includes. How many servings of tea and coffee does it include? It may only be two, in which case you may need to order another serving for registration. Is the lunch price for a finger buffet, fork buffet or a more formal seated meal? How many courses?

## Considering drinks

Are soft drinks included in the price? If not, what are the costs? Very often the soft drinks such as mineral water and orange juice are charged per bottle or carton used, so you only pay for what you use. If this is the case it is important to give the caterers a limit so that they notify you when it has been reached. The amount can add up very quickly and work out very costly if you do not control it.

These days delegates tend not to expect wine with their meal as was traditionally the case. Hotels may have their own bar as well as having a temporary bar facility in the conference area. Many organisers opt to let delegates purchase their own drinks at the hotel bar rather than having the temporary one opened. Sober delegates make for much happier delegates and the after-lunch slump is made many times worse if delegates have been drinking alcohol. If wine is to be served it will be charged at premium rates and it can be false economy to provide your own. The corkage charge made by the venue for every bottle opened may result in you paying even more.

### Reducing catering costs

Some organisers have the luxury of working with a large budget and minimum restriction on catering and other costs. More common, though, is the organiser with a limited budget who is still required to provide the best of everything.

If you are working to a restricted budget and are finding it difficult to make ends meet there are a few compromises that can be made.

◆ Question whether you need to serve biscuits with each serving of tea and coffee. If not, this could be a worthwhile saving and is especially practical if a sweet is being included in the lunch.

◆ A buffet lunch will always be more cost effective than a seated lunch. Select the items carefully, e.g. a wholesome lasagne and jacket potato will be both filling and cost effective.

◆ Check whether you are to be charged room hire for the use of the lunch room. Often if you are having catering there will be no room hire charge, however this is not always the case and it is an area that may be open to negotiation.

◆ Issue delegates with vouchers to exchange for tea/coffee and lunch. Agree to pay the caterers according to the number of vouchers collected. This ensures you only pay for what is consumed and can represent a significant saving.

◆ Consider if packed (boxed) lunches might be acceptable.

## NEGOTIATING RATES

Do not be inhibited about negotiating the room rates. Venues do not come with immovable price tags attached. They will have a rack rate which is the full quoted price, but very often this is the starting price and there is almost always some room for manoeuvre. Start at a price lower than you would expect them to accept so that a compromise will lead you to a more realistic target. Don't forget, if you start high you cannot get lower. Although you will probably be asked directly, avoid telling them exactly what your budget is. Keep it as vague as possible to start with, 'This is being run on a tight budget'; 'We have a reasonable budget but it is likely we will still require some compromise on both our parts'. Appear cool and confident when negotiating. However much you may like this particular venue, remember there are many alternative venues you could use, and the venue co-ordinator will be aware of that.

If you are preparing a series of conferences around the country you may also be able to gain an extra discount by using a hotel chain that will give a discount for multiple bookings.

If you do not feel that you can negotiate well, ask the venue-finding agency to do it on your behalf. They are very experienced at such things and may already have a discount arrangement.

## What to look for

The 'package' that will be offered can vary hugely between one venue and the next. All have their advantages and disadvantages and the benefits must be weighed up considering the type of event you are organising. As a rule, purpose-built training centres often have more equipment included in the room hire rate than most hotels. This can include whiteboards, TV and video monitors and other audio visual equipment. Some venues may include an organiser's office, the speaker room, the lectern, staging and tables in their price.

## Paying professionals

It is likely that you will need to bring in other event professionals at some point during the preparation for and the running of the event. Printers, audio visual technicians, stage designers and freelance organisers have their own rates and these should be made clear from the start. Establish whether expenses are to be added on to their basic fee and establish payment terms.

## Playing safe

Ensure a contingency fund is built into the budget. This will cover unforeseen expenses and will help to ensure that your budget does not get out of control.

## ARRANGING SPONSORSHIP

Having decided to seek sponsorship in one form or another from one or more companies, draw up a list of companies and/or organisations that would benefit from reaching the type of delegates that you are hoping to attract yourself.

The benefit to sponsors is the opportunity to communicate directly with potential customers, to raise their company profile whilst meeting their marketing objectives. The benefit to you is that they will be paying for the privilege and so providing some often much needed cash.

Your options are to obtain either full sponsorship from one company, or to break down the various elements that could be sponsored and offer them to a variety of organisations.

## Looking at sponsorship opportunities

You are limited only by your imagination when it comes to thinking of items to have sponsored. From biros to baseball caps, from balloons to briefcases, there will be a promotional gift company that will be able to satisfy your needs. There are currently at least two major trade shows dedicated to the incentive and promotional gift market. Take a trip to one of these and you will be able to discuss your requirements in detail with suppliers, and gather ideas and examples from the items on display. You may also be able to take advantage of special show offers giving you a significant discount on your orders.

### Knowing what to charge sponsors

Draw up a list of items you think would be appropriate to your event and work out the cost of those items to be produced, including the screen-print charge and delivery. Then add on a percentage which is the sponsor's contribution to the event. The amount will vary according to your particular circumstances. (When calculating the cost of the screen-printing be aware of the increase in charges if using more than one colour.)

## How to contact potential sponsors

Circulate a letter of introduction and a sponsorship form to your list of potential sponsors, making sure it looks professional and attractive. Ensure that it clearly stresses the benefits to the organisation should they decide to take up the opportunity. Be totally honest about the expected number of delegates, mailing, numbers of brochures, etc. Include a date by which forms should be returned, and be sure to enclose a contact name and telephone number for any queries.

## Confirming the sponsorship agreement

Having obtained an initial agreement to sponsor the event, send a written sponsorship agreement, making it clear exactly what is included in the package, confirming the cost, and informing them of the date that the invoice will be sent and the terms of payment. This ensures that it is clear from the start that there is no room for misinterpretation. Sponsors should be invoiced before the relevant items are ordered, so that should they have a last minute change of heart you are not left to pick up the bill for 200 delegate bags with their logo printed on them.

Logos are designed at great expense and play an important part in a company's corporate identity. It is essential that designs for your sponsored items are approved by the company.

## TAKING CARE OF SPONSORS

Having provided the financial resources to enable you to hold your event it is worth looking after your sponsors. Without them the financial outlay could render the event unviable and, of course, you may wish to approach them

## Carpet Manufacturers Association

### Autumn Conference

| Item | Benefits | Cost | Confirm choice | Please call to discuss |
|------|----------|------|----------------|------------------------|
| Delegate bags (linen shoulder bags) | ● High visibility<br>● Post-event use<br>● Includes 2 free delegate places | £1,000<br>200 bags | | |
| Notebooks and pens | ● Continued use provides visual reminder | £750<br>200 A4 notebooks<br>200 boxed pens | | |
| Delegate pack inserts | ● Provides cost-effective marketing opportunity to targeted decision makers | £250<br>200 A4 flyers required by 20th September | | |
| Programme advertisement – ½ page | ● Association with quality event | £150<br>CRC to be received by 1st September | | |
| Programme advertisement – whole page | ● Association with quality event | £200<br>CRC to be received by 1st September | | |

All sponsorship opportunities include sponsors' logo on the conference brochure. Prices are exclusive of screen print charge and VAT. Total cost will be confirmed at time of booking.

Name:

Position:

Company:

Address:

Tel:                               Fax:                               Email:

Please return this form to Jim May at the Carpet Manufacturers Association, Carpet House, 73 Brighton Road, Bournemouth. Tel: 01412 334556.

Fig. 14. Sponsorship opportunity form.

23rd January 200X

Mr A Wilson
Wildlife Magazine
22 York Road
Dover

Dear Mr Wilson

Thank you for agreeing to sponsor the West Midlands Nature Centre's Conference 'A Walk on the Wild Side' to be held on 22nd May.

I would like to confirm that you have chosen the option of sponsored notebooks and pens which will be placed inside the delegate packs. This option also includes two free places at the conference. An invoice for the agreed sum of £750 will follow under separate cover.

Please forward a bromide or tiff file of your company logo, along with any guidelines for its placement. I will send a copy of the notebook design incorporating your logo for your approval as soon as possible.

I am sure that you will find this a worthwhile opportunity and look forward to speaking to you again in due course.

Yours sincerely

Fig. 15. Sponsorship confirmation letter.

again in future years. In terms of physical products – pens, bags, brochures, etc – send a set to the sponsor when they have been produced. In the case of brochures that carry their logo, you may find that the sponsor is willing to distribute brochures on your behalf as it can be of mutual benefit.

## After the event
After the event send a personalised thank you letter to the sponsor. If the delegate list was to be part of the sponsorship agreement, ensure this is also sent promptly (first checking this does not contravene data protection legislation.)

## Sponsorship ideas
◆ advertisement in brochure
◆ dinner
◆ wine
◆ cocktail reception
◆ flowers
◆ luncheons/bags/documentation
◆ pens/badges
◆ notepads
◆ signs
◆ conference speaker expenses
◆ carpet tiles
◆ banners
◆ breakfasts
◆ menus.

# 8

# Assessing the Audio Visual Requirements

*'Different events and different speakers have specific audio visual requirements.'*

It is important that you establish early on in the planning process what is available in the venue of your choice, what each speaker's requirements are, and the costs involved. Do not take for granted the condition and quality if using in-house equipment. Without a specialist to look after it the equipment may be out-dated, have intermittent faults or be of low quality.

## LOOKING AT THE CHOICE OF VISUAL PROJECTION

Traditionally presentations were given with the aid of an **overhead projector (OHP)** or by **slide projection** (35mm). These are still used today, but becoming more popular are computer generated presentations, made by commonly available software to produce an assortment of visual imagery, such as Powerpoint.

The benefit of a more technical presentation in terms of projection equipment, when used well, is dramatically increased visual stimulation for the delegates. The down side is that the more sophisticated equipment involved, the more room there could be for error, which could, in the worst case scenario, result in a flustered speaker with no visual aids and a room full of bored and restless delegates. However, as data projectors are now mainstream and compatibility issues with PCs and laptops are minimal, problems are far less likely.

## Computer generated graphics/Powerpoint

Software is readily available which enables a presentation to be generated on a personal computer and then digitally projected onto a standard projection screen. The result can be extremely effective, and can include audio as well as visual effects. Photographs, text, diagrams and computer generated imagery can be combined to make interesting and memorable presentations. Unfortunately even more memorable is when such a presentation breaks down, and it is vital to ensure that the technician or person in charge of the AV is aware of the version of software that has been used to create it. This is to ensure that the computer, leads and cables are compatible. It is also possible, and preferable, to transfer the presentation in advance on to a disk, CD Rom, memory stick or have the presentation forwarded by email, so that it can be loaded onto the event computer that has been preloaded with the appropriate software.

## Video projection

Presenters may wish to use video footage to illustrate their talk. A television and a standard domestic video recorder would be unsuitable for any more than a very few delegates. Alternatives are to use either a very large monitor, which may be impractical, a 'video wall' which could be costly, or to simply have the video feed plugged into a video/data projector so that the video image can be projected onto a normal screen.

Video tapes come in different formats (VHS, Super VHS, High-Band U-Matic or Betacam which is broadcast quality). Be sure that you ascertain the format and inform the supplier of the video equipment.

**Slide projection**
35 mm slides (also sometimes called transparencies) can be still photographs, drawings, diagrams, text, etc.

*Your options*
- Using a **dissolve unit** makes it possible to use two projectors consecutively, allowing one image to fade out as another fades in, making for a very smooth transition.

- Other sophisticated techniques are also available and your AV technician will be able to discuss your requirements and advise on the options currently available.

- The projector can be operated manually or using cable or an infra-red remote control. The remote control allows the speaker to remain at his/her presentation point and move the slides on when required.

*Types of slide*
It is wise to encourage speakers to use glass-mounted slides if possible. Slides that are not glass-mounted can be affected by the heat of the lamp if the projector is in constant use and can also get caught in the projector. An argument is sometimes raised regarding glass mounts,

that if dropped or damaged in transit the broken glass can pierce the slide, damaging the slide irreparably. This is a valid point, but one that has to be weighed up against the same slide being damaged in the projector. Glass replacement slide mounts can be purchased in all good camera shops and it is possible to re-mount slides already produced using plastic mounts.

*Other practicalities*
It is useful for speakers to number their slides and to stick a coloured dot on the top of each one so that in the unfortunate case of a carousel being dropped (not an uncommon occurrence) they can be put back in the same order and up the correct way with ease.

'Blackout' (darkening of the room) will be essential for the slides to be effective. If using front projection the projector and stand will be placed between the rows of seats, the distance between the projector and screen being dictated by the size of image required and the size of the projector lens.

*Front and back projection*
Images from a data or slide projector can be projected onto a screen either

◆ in front of the screen: front projection
◆ or from behind the screen: back or rear projection.

Back projection looks neater as the projector does not need to be placed in the middle of the room, between the rows of seats, but it does require space behind the screen which can cut down the room's seating capacity. It is important to inform speakers if back projection is to be used if using 35mm slides they will need to be loaded in the correct order but back to front.

### Overhead projector (OHP)

Clear acetate sheets (also called transparencies) are placed over a light-box which is then magnified and projected on to the screen. The height of the projection can be altered, as can the clarity of the image. The transparencies can be prepared in advance by the speaker, or if, for example, asking for examples or comments from the audience, they can be written on during the talk using special fibre tip pens in an assortment of colours. Graphics can be produced onto acetate as well as text, and with the aid of a simple word processor and/or desk top publishing software profes-sional-looking transparencies can be created.

The OHP needs to be located in front of the screen and cannot be operated remotely, therefore it can be distracting for the audience. An OHP is more commonly used in lecture/academic presentations where the style of delivery of the presentation is less critical. If using an OHP, a spare bulb is essential.

## SOUND SYSTEMS AND RELATED ITEMS

Obviously it is essential that the delegates can hear the speakers. Be aware that the ability of sound to be absorbed and reflected means that the acoustics of an empty or full room will be quite different. **Ambient** (existing) noise, including the air conditioning unit if present, should be at a minimum, and the room should not be subject to external disturbances.

## To ensure the speaker can be heard

*Microphones*
Through the use of a microphone an amplifier allows the volume of the speaker's voice/presentation aids to be adjusted to suitable levels. Some people who are generally softly spoken will be unable to project their voice very far without sounding like they are shouting, so it is essential that a sound system is in place.

Microphones can be hand-held, or more usually placed on an adjustable stand. They can also be placed on 'table-top' stands.

*Radio and roving mikes*
Some speakers, especially those who naturally tend to be more animated or who like to move around the stage, will be better suited to a radio mike which can be a tie-clip or hand-held microphone, which transmits the radio signal to the amplifier. In a similar way you could use the cordless radio or roving mike which can be passed around the audience at question time. As these microphones are battery powered, ensure you have spare batteries available.

A word of warning about using roving mikes – it is useful if one of your staff can 'control' its whereabouts as it is passed around the audience so that any delegates with an axe to grind or someone who is going off at a tangent cannot get hold of it and refuse to let go.

*Hiring equipment*
Many purpose-built conference venues and hotels have

amplifiers already situated in their conference rooms, and microphones can be hired from them at minimal cost. If, however, the room does not contain a sound system, check the cost of hiring one when evaluating the venue as the additional cost may be prohibitive.

### Lecterns
A lectern is a stand for holding scripts, prompt cards, microphone, etc whilst the presenter is speaking. They come in an assortment of shapes and sizes, from a basic stand to one that contains a control panel for lights, the projector, the sound system, etc. They will usually have a light attached to illuminate the speaker's notes when the main lights are dimmed. It is useful to place a small, easily read clock on the lectern to enable the speaker to keep an eye on the time without having to look at his/her watch. If the lectern does contain a control panel ensure that the speakers and chairperson have been fully briefed as to its use.

If the venue cannot provide a suitable lectern an AV company will be able to supply one to suit your needs.

### OPERATING THE EQUIPMENT
The AV technician (or operator) is an important player in the staging of an event. You need to decide who is going to take on the role. Options include one of your own staff or associates who has some knowledge of the systems being used. Alternatively you could use the services of a professional technician.

## Choosing between professional and non-professional technicians

| | Non-professional | Professional technician |
|---|---|---|
| ◆ Benefits | Minimum cost | Professional charge (from £150 per day) Experienced and quickly effective in case of breakdown Able to supply additional equipment as required Carries spare bulbs, batteries etc as required May be familiar with the venue |
| ◆ Drawbacks | May not be able to cope in breakdown situation If concentrating on equipment will not be able to participate in conference Workload/stress during event will spoil person's enjoyment of the event. | Financial implication |

# CONTRACTING AN AUDIO VISUAL COMPANY

Audio visual companies advertise their services in many trade magazines and can also be found locally in the *Yellow Pages*. Venue staff can also recommend local companies who are familiar with their venue.

It is worthwhile obtaining quotes from different AV companies before making a final decision, but be aware not to go by cost alone, experience is also very important. You are not only looking for a company who is within your budget (don't forget you could get sponsorship to cover the AV costs) but also someone you feel confident would be cool and effective in a crisis.

Audio visual companies can also provide stage sets, walk-in/background music, lighting, autocues and more.

OUR ENVIRONMENT, OUR FUTURE CONFERENCE
Wednesday, 12th May 200X

**AUDIO VISUAL REQUIREMENTS FORM**
to be returned by 20th April 200X

Speaker's Name:
Title of Presentation:
Date/Time:

I understand that my audio visual requirements as listed below will be provided. I also note that additional equipment will not be available unless previously specified.

Please tick . . .

| | |
|---|---|
| 35mm slides | ☐ |
| OHP | ☐ |
| Video | ☐ specify exact format ................. |
| Powerpoint | ☐ specify exact version ................. |
| | from your own laptop   yes/no |
| | VGA/SVGA |

Signed .....................................................

It is intended that, with your permission, the presentations will be recorded on audio tape and will then be available for purchase by delegates and other parties. Please confirm whether you give you consent for this to take place (*delete as appropriate*).

■ I confirm that my presentation may be recorded and distributed.
■ I do not wish for my presentation to be recorded and distributed.

Signed .....................................................

Fig. 16. Audio visual request form.

# 9

# Staging the Event

*'You will need adequate staff to make the day run smoothly.'*

## STAFFING THE EVENT

At the absolute minimum you will need at least one extra pair of hands at the registration desk in case you are called away to trouble-shoot. The desk should be manned at all times throughout the registration period and afterwards in case of late comers.

A briefing to all staff members in advance of the first delegates arriving will ensure that they are aware of the location of toilets, cloakroom facilities and lunch room, and of time schedules and other important details.

### Assessing staffing requirements

You will need adequate staff to make the day run smoothly. Before the event, ask yourself these questions:

- Who is going to switch the house lights on and off?
- Who is going to operate the projector?
- Who is going to pass around the roving mike?
- Who is going to deal with press enquiries?

If the conference is spread over a large campus, do you need directional staff at strategic points?

*Meeting staff needs*

If you do not have adequate staff readily available, you can often summon up help from various places. These could include:

♦ Local students if the venue is a university and the subject being discussed is appropriate to their area of study. Very often students, always on a tight budget, will appreciate free entry to the conference in exchange for tasks such as looking after the lights.

♦ Volunteers from your club/association.

♦ You can also hire professional conference staff from specialist agencies – obviously a costly option but worthwhile in terms of experience compared to the previous options.

Staff, whether voluntary or hired, must be smartly dressed in keeping with the image you wish to project. Badges or sashes will help delegates identify staff.

## BEFORE THE DAY STARTS

Before anyone arrives walk the route from the car park or entrance to the registration desk and on to the conference room. Imagine you are arriving for the first time, as your delegates will be shortly. Is the route clearly signposted? Are there any recently-placed obstacles blocking the route? Is it clean and tidy? Sort out the problem immediately if necessary. This may mean doing it yourself or asking venue staff to take care of it.

Test (or witness) the audio visual equipment being used yourself to make sure all is working properly.

## Briefing staff and delegates

Ensure that all key personnel are briefed in relation to evacuation procedures and any other related matters, and that the emergency exists are identified and kept clear. Their location and the congregation point outside the building should be clearly described to delegates during the chairperson's opening remarks.

# DEALING WITH REGISTRATION

The registration desk should be sited where it is going to be easily spotted as delegates arrive, and where delegates are not able to slip through without registering. The desk should be kept free of junk – remember this is the first impression that delegates will have of the event. First impressions should not be underestimated. If you have access to display boards, two or three placed behind the desk will look professional, provide an opportunity to display the event or your organisation logo, and also provide somewhere behind which to store things.

If delegates are required to register and collect conference bags someone should be free to deal with queries which may arise, such as late payments, so as to avoid holding up the rest of the queue.

Often on your arrival you will be met by the venue co-ordinator who will run through the day's events with you. You should have the means to contact this person should a query or emergency arise during the event. This could be via walkie-talkie, phone or pager.

## The purpose of badges

Badges are very useful for a number of reasons. As well as

allowing immediate identification for security reasons they also encourage networking. For example, at an international conference very few people may know each other and placing the country of origin as well as the delegate's name on the badge can help to break the ice.

There are various options available. You can choose from a variety of materials including stickers, rigid plastic or the more common PVC badge holder with a card inserted into it. These come in a wide assortment of styles, sizes and prices. You can have badges pre-printed by a specialist badge company or you can print the delegates' names on labels and stick them onto a card printed with the event logo which can then be inserted into a badge holder.

*Badge layouts*
Depending on the type of conference, you can choose the layout that is most appropriate. At business events it is usual to include the delegate's name, position and company, but there are no hard and fast rules for this. Other ideas follows:

| name | name | name | name |
|------|------|------|------|
|      | company | position | company |
|      |         | company | country |

Badges can be attached to clothing by a pin or a clip. Ladies may prefer a pin as they typically do not have a breast pocket on suits. Tape **lanyards** are becoming increasingly popular allowing the delegates to hang the badge around their necks. The badges themselves and the neck cord offer another opportunity for sponsorship. The size of the font used on the badges must be large enough for the details to be read at a reasonable distance. This avoids delegates having to stand six inches away from the next delegate whilst staring at their bosom in order to read their name badge!

## PREPARING DELEGATE PACKS

You may intend giving each delegate an information pack as they arrive. It may include a programme or itinerary, speaker biographies, abstracts of the presentations, a delegate list and any sponsored items such as pens, notebooks and advertising material. The pack may be a simple cardboard folder, a cloth bag, or even a small briefcase. The options are numerous and, of course, provide an excellent sponsorship opportunity. They should be packed in advance of the event as it can be a time-consuming and laborious job.

## REMEMBERING DELEGATE CARE

You will want to create the best possible learning environment for your delegates, and that includes making them feel relaxed and welcome. Delegates who travel from some distance often over-estimate how long it will take to get there, so expect them early.

You and your staff should remain helpful, cheerful and understanding throughout the event – but not patronising, especially if delegates arrive stressed after a difficult journey.

### Coping with grievances

If a delegate has a grievance for any reason, take them

away from the main registration area to discuss it. The benefits of this are:

1. You can give them your full attention.
2. They will feel you are listening to them.
3. Other delegates need not be affected by it.

Whether or not the complaint is justified, keep calm. Keep your voice steady and listen fully to what the person has to say. Obtain the facts of the matter, empathise with the complainant and assure them that you have understood their complaint. Be sure that any action promised to resolve the situation is taken and followed up as necessary.

In any situation where a query or grievance is made that cannot be dealt with immediately, assure the delegate that you will get the information or explanation they need as soon as possible (and don't forget to do it!)

## Making registration smooth

Keep queues as short as possible. If the registration period is reasonably long you will find delegates arrive at varying times which makes the registration process much easier, as opposed to a 15-minute registration period for 200 people when they will all arrive at the same time. If delegate bags, papers, badges, etc are to be issued, work out a system in advance so that it runs as smoothly as possible.

### Providing an appropriate atmosphere

Providing coffee and tea during registration helps delegates to settle down after their journey before the conference starts and also helps to create a networking environment. Many venues include coffee on arrival in the day-delegate price – but do not take this for granted. Remember to check and order in advance if necessary.

## Taking messages
It is useful to have a message board next to the registration desk. Telephone messages for delegates that come in during the day can be pinned on to it. You should be able to obtain the telephone number of the registration desk in advance of the event. If so, it can be useful to issue it to delegates in the confirmation letter, together with a reminder that mobile phones must be switched off or turned to silent/vibrate whilst the conference is in session.

## Contacting other services
Keep contact details for the local doctor, hospital, taxi and railway enquiry office in an accessible place as you will be bound to be asked for at least one of them. Also take along a tool box full of useful items, such as scissors and sellotape, that may be required.

## Giving notice of time
If the day is going to run to schedule, it is essential that it starts on time. Give the delegates notice when the event is due to start, first ten minutes, then five minutes, then when it starts – there are always stragglers! When the delegates are all safely stowed in their room, tidy up the registration area in preparation for the morning break. Check the toilets to see if they are clean and tidy, and adequately stocked and alert the venue staff if they are not.

## Looking after everyone

During the refreshment breaks, don't forget to look after those people who often get waylaid, such as the chairperson and the audio visual technicians. They will be as in need of refreshment as everyone else, but often find themselves tied up with delegates and other speakers.

## Refreshment breaks

After the first refreshment break, assess how it went – were there long queues? Was there enough coffee? If there had been any problem alert the appropriate person (e.g. the venue staff) so that the later refreshment breaks can be trouble-free. Waiting time for tea and coffee can be reduced by ensuring that the number of serving points are adequate for the number of delegates. One serving point for 150 delegates is going to result in considerably longer queues than three or four serving points. A useful tip is to have the milk sugar and biscuits on a separate table so that delegates move away from the serving area as swiftly as possible.

## Lunch provision

If providing lunch for exhibitors, they will appreciate being able to have it prior to the delegates breaking for lunch. This must be pre-arranged with caterers and will result in stands being fully manned during breaks. The menu for lunch will have been decided upon some time before. If tables and chairs are not available in the lunch room, order a fork, or more preferably, a finger buffet so that delegates will be able to eat it easily. Most venues have a range of menus to suit a variety of budgets and seating arrangements and will be able to give advice based on their experience.

## REMEMBERING SPEAKER CARE

Even experienced speakers can suffer from nerves before presenting, and this is no bad thing as the resulting increase in adrenalin often helps to boost the speaker's performance. There are certain steps, though, that can be taken to prevent the speakers becoming unnecessarily stressed. As mentioned in the chapter on choosing speakers, you should have provided the speakers with adequate directions to the venue and instructions as to what to do on arrival, such as whether they need to register with you and collect a badge, or whether they need to report to another person. If your budget and the facilities allow, it is useful to have a separate room for the speakers' use, where they can prepare themselves, run through their slides and generally get away from the hustle and bustle of the main conference area.

Before their talk is not the time to discuss payments and other details. Wait until after the presentation so that the speakers can remain focused on the job in hand.

### Checking arrangements

*   By requesting each speaker's estimated time of arrival and method of transport in advance you will be in a position to know whether there is any cause for concern if a speaker has not arrived at the start of the conference. Other commitments may prevent them from attending the whole event and you will expend much-needed energy and resources chasing missing speakers who may have had no intention of arriving until lunchtime for their afternoon talk.

| ITEMS TO TAKE ALONG IN YOUR 'TOOL BOX' | |
|---|---|
| – Velcro hoops/hooks | – Tape measure |
| – Blu-tak | – Chalk |
| – Sellotape | – A nail file |
| – Masking tape | – Spare badge holders |
| – Spare batteries | – Scissors |
| – Pencils and pens | – Staples and stapler |
| – Rubber bands | – Phonecards |
| – Cloakroom tickets | – 10p coins |
| – Safety pins | – Coins for parking meters |
| – A needle and thread | – A gentleman's tie |
| – Drawing pins | – Mints |

Fig. 17. Tool box contents list.

◆ If visual aids are being used, introduce the speaker to the operator so that necessary information can be exchanged and time can be arranged for setting up their particular AV system.

◆ Don't forget the chairperson when dealing with speaker issues. Ensure they have been introduced to the day's speakers and that they have appropriate biographies to enable them to introduce them. They should also have a list of any 'housekeeping' notices they need to give, such as any health and safety instructions, lunch notices, etc.

◆ If you are in the luxurious position of having some or all of the speakers arriving for rehearsals prior to the event (perhaps whilst you are setting up the day before) allocate each of them a time slot so that they are aware that you will be working to a schedule. It is unfortunately not uncommon to set up a rehearsal afternoon and for all of the speakers to turn up expecting the technician's undivided attention during the final half-hour.

◆ Bottled mineral water or a jug of fresh water and glasses should be available on or close to the lectern for the speakers and chairperson. One of the symptoms of nerves is a dry throat, so make sure that lubrication is within easy reach!

## TROUBLE-SHOOTING

In the event of a disaster – the screen falls over, the sound system breaks down, a speaker fails to arrive – *stay calm*! Everyone will look to you for the answer; it is not the incident that will be remembered – it is how quickly you get things back together.

At the end of the day, don't forget to have a look around for any belongings that have been left behind by delegates. You will often find a jumper, an umbrella and someone's delegate bag containing their scrupulously taken notes. As the delegates are leaving all staff must be courteous and make the delegates feel that their presence has been appreciated.

### Enjoying yourself

Above all, enjoy the event! Delegates, speakers and management will all take their cue from you as the key person. If you appear relaxed, cheerful but alert and ready to respond to any emergency, so will they. Conversely, if you appear nervous, anxious and look upon the whole event as a burden rather than a challenge, no one will enjoy it.

# 10

# Obtaining Press Coverage

*'Press coverage can be useful to highlight particular topics of general interest, encourage people to attend and to give an extra incentive to sponsors.'*

## SELECTING THE APPROPRIATE MEDIA

### Trade press
Specialist journals targeted at particular interest groups. These journals are often keen to include events which would appeal to their readers. They may also wish to send a representative along to write a report of the event in a later edition.

### National press
Broadsheet and tabloid newspapers. The story needs to have strong general interest and be particularly topical. Many specialist supplements, have a regular 'What's On' listing and even if you cannot obtain any editorial space, if the subject is relevant you should not have any problem getting it listed.

### Local press
Evening, daily, weekly and free papers. These papers focus on stories of interest to the local community and can be targeted from three angles as in the examples below.

*Locality of delegates*
'Local people are being encouraged to attend the West Cumbria Conservation Conference that is being held at the Diglis Sports Centre on 30th October. Many people relocate to West Cumbria because of the beautiful countryside, but to secure its beauty for future generations we are all being encouraged to think ahead and to support schemes set up by the Conservation Trust that will be discussed . . .'

*Locality of the event*
'Bradshaw on Sea is delighted to be hosting the 2005 International Lacemaking Conference. The event, being run by the Bradshaw Lacemaking Circle, will attract delegates from across the world to hear speakers discussing the latest techniques and designs.'

*Locality of speaker*
'Dingford's Mayoress, Mrs Jean Smith, will be travelling to Cardiff on Saturday to address a conference aimed at reducing Local Government spending. Using Dingford as an example, Mrs Smith will discuss how smaller towns can flourish with creative spending.'

## National radio
BBC and independent radio stations. As with national newspapers, the story needs to have strong appeal to catch the imagination of the radio producers/commissioning editors who will be inundated with press releases on a daily basis. By reading a copy of the *Radio* or *TV Times* it is easy to identify which programmes are devoted to particular issues – always send the press release to a particular show producer or editor, not just addressed to

the radio station. A telephone call to the appropriate radio station is all that is needed to establish the programme producer's contact details.

### Local radio
Local BBC and independent radio stations. Local radio, as local newspapers, need a continuance of stories about local people/issues, so try to target them from all three angles shown for local papers.

## WRITING THE PRESS RELEASE
Remember that you are not only requiring the attention of the eventual newspaper readers, but that of the journalist him/herself who has to be persuaded to use the press release as a basis for an article. Editors and radio producers receive many press releases on a daily basis, so yours must stand out from the crowd. To do that you need a 'hook' to catch their attention.

### Creating the copy
1. Ideally one A4 page should be adequate.

2. Many people will not read further than the first paragraph, so you have to be able to get your message across succinctly before going on to fill in the details in later paragraphs.

3. Type on one side of the paper only, use double line spacing, ensure it is dated at the top and has 'Ends' at the foot of the copy.

4. Under the main body of text put notes for the editor, such as contact name and telephone number for further details, enclosures, etc. It may also be useful to note

which, if any, of your speakers are 'media friendly', i.e. are comfortable, articulate and possibly experienced at talking to the media.

5.  Include a quote from a spokesperson if appropriate.

6.  Make the headline short and snappy, and avoid jargon and acronyms.

7.  Include who, what, why and how.

8.  Enclose photo(s) of speaker(s) and the conference brochure.

See Figure 18 for an example.

## LOOKING AFTER THE JOURNALISTS

Always include details of how journalists can attend. Usually members of the press attend events free of charge, and in return publish articles on the conference. Ensure that they receive directions and instructions as to where to go on arrival. Remember that editorial space which journalists can provide would cost thousands of pounds if you had to pay for it in a national newspaper so it is a sound investment to put in the effort.

## PROVIDING A PRESS ROOM

Depending on the profile of the event and if you are expecting high media interest, you may need to consider whether you will require a press room on-site for the duration of the conference. In here, you should provide any information that may be of interest to the media, including details of sponsors and exhibitors if appropriate. You should also provide:

---

**PRESS RELEASE**

Date: 5 May 200X

**Capacity Crowd as Buxford Sports Club Goes for Gold!!**

Over 150 people converged on the White Hart Hotel in Buxford at the weekend for a conference aimed at looking at how local sports clubs can contribute to the Government's on-going programme to create an abundance of world-class athletes to compete for the country at a professional level.

Delegates from sports clubs as far afield as Cornwall and Midlothian listened to speakers including the Sports Minister, the Right Hon Joe Bloggs (picture enclosed), who discussed the current situation and case studies of several projects that are running in some areas of the country.

Sponsored by Buxford's own Manglow Sports Superstore, the conference is set to become an annual event and next year the organisers are hoping to include a series of workshops and an exhibition to run alongside the conference.

'Buxford Sports Club should be proud of this initiative,' said an enthusiastic Mr Bloggs, 'with this sort of enthusiasm I am sure the new training programmes will soon be paying off and Britain will again be on the world map as far as athletics are concerned.'

**Ends**

Note for editors: For further details please contact Cathy Pritchard on 01234 56789. Enclosed: Photo of Rt Hon Joe Bloggs speaking at the 'Going for Gold' conference on 2nd May 200X

---

Fig 18. Press release. (Please note text should be double spaced.)

- a phone
- fax machine
- modem point
- coffee/refreshments
- seating.

If your budget will not stretch to a press room (remember to include room hire, phone charges, fax hire and refreshments in your budget), you can at least provide your press delegates with a folder including items pertaining to the cause of the event, biographies of speakers, literature from event sponsors and contact details for more information.

## POST-CONFERENCE PUBLICITY

If you are unable to generate outside interest before and during the event, write your own review or press release afterwards for circulation to appropriate media. To add interest you can include quotes from satisfied delegates, and good quality photos of the conference in progress. As well as creating possible post-conference publicity, it will also alert the journalists to attend on another occasion.

# (11)

# Exhibitors and Exhibitions

*'The financial value of the exhibition industry is substantial.'*

## THE EXHIBITION INDUSTRY

Exhibitions can be divided into **trade shows** and **consumer shows**:

◆ Trade shows are aimed at particular segments of industry or markets, such as the library industry or the security industry.

◆ Consumer shows are targeted at the end-user and as such are open to the general public, such as the Ideal Home Exhibition or the Boat Show.

Some exhibitions may run for several days, and have different days dedicated to the press, trade and the public. Stand-holders, or exhibitors, purchase space to display their wares or services alongside others. The exhibition companies provide the venue and facilities and aim to sell a required amount of exhibition space and to draw in as many visitors to the exhibition as possible to view those stands.

Becoming increasingly popular are consumer shows related to popular television programmes or magazines, such as The Clothes Show Live and the GQ ACTIVE Show. These enable members of the public to 'experience' the concept and participate in demonstrations, meet the presenters, etc.

## Conferences and exhibitions

Large exhibitions are a separate part of the events industry and guidelines for running them are not within the scope of this book. However, many conferences do have exhibitors in one form or another to complement the conference, just as some exhibitions include a conference. In most cases the exhibition at a conference will consists of a handful of stands, some may have many more, but the emphasis is on the conference as the main event with exhibitors being welcome additions. However, the fact that the exhibition may be of secondary importance does not mean that it should be thrown together without due consideration and planning.

> Just as you would wish for the conference to be the best it could possibly be, the same should be true for the exhibition.

## INCORPORATING AN EXHIBITION IN YOUR CONFERENCE

### Why should we have exhibitors?

There are benefits to be gained by everyone if an exhibition is to be included in the conference agenda.

*Benefits to the organisers*
♦ Income generation from sale of stand space.

*Benefits to the delegates*
- Increased interest.
- Opportunity to talk directly to suppliers.

*Benefits to the exhibitors*
- Captive audience of potential customers.

## SOURCING EXHIBITORS

As with sourcing potential sponsors, draw up a list of companies/organisations which would identify your delegates as potential customers. It would be sensible for the option to exhibit to be included in the sponsorship form.

Having identified, contacted and reached an agreement with an exhibitor, confirm the arrangement in writing, detailing exactly what the package includes, what the cost will be and when the invoice will be issued.

## WHAT TO INCLUDE IN THE COST

Some exhibitors use their own portable stands and will require only the space in which to erect it. However, this is by no means always the case and you should indicate whether furniture will be included, such as tables, cloths and chairs. As it is likely that these will be provided by the venue at no cost to yourself they should be included. Other furniture and display boards or shell schemes could be provided to order and invoiced for directly by the supplier.

Free delegate places to the actual conference will again not cost you anything other than the catering costs, so including a couple of places in the package will be seen as a benefit, and also make it clear that the places are limited and that it will not be possible for more stand staff to wander in and out as they please.

## Shell schemes

Shell schemes can enhance the appearance of an exhibition by keeping the overall design of the stands the same. A combination of aluminium framework and panels of various materials, shell schemes can be supplied by specialist companies and can include a fascia board which allows company names and stand numbers to be displayed. Some panels are covered in a velcro-compatible loop nylon which allows graphics to be easily attached.

## ALLOCATING SPACE

Obtain a detailed floor plan of the exhibition area, including power points and telephone points. Mark on potential exhibitor spaces. Look at where the premium sites may be. Delegates will tend to congregate:

◆ close to the coffee serving point
◆ immediately opposite the entrance to the exhibition
◆ on the main thoroughfares.

As exhibitors confirm their places the floor plan can also be confirmed and should be passed to the venue staff for approval. They will need to ensure that the layout meets with their Health and Safety requirements in terms of keeping emergency exits clear. The shell scheme contractors, if used, and anyone else involved in the construction of the exhibition stands, should be supplied with a copy of the floor plan.

Before the exhibitors arrive to set up, measure out the individual stand spaces and mark them up with chalk or masking tape. It may be that you are providing exhibition carpeting, in which case it may be possible to use a different colour carpeting for the stand areas to the rest of the floor.

The exhibitors should be provided with clear instructions and it can be helpful to provide them with an exhibitor pack or manual, similar to the speaker packs.

## The exhibitor information pack

*Background information on your organisation*
They may be unfamiliar with the aims and objectives of your organisation and this will help them to understand 'where you are coming from'.

*Overview of event*
The aims and objectives of the event and a very brief history if it has run before.

*Details of the exhibition*
When it will run and the number and duration of the opportunities the delegates will have to visit the exhibition.

*Details of the conference programme*
They may have items that are pertinent to particular presentations.

*Documents*
1. What is required from them in terms of company description for the programme (including the maximum number of words to be used).

2. A form for the exhibitors to complete and return that confirms they will abide by all relevant Health and Safety requirements and that they have carried out a risk assessment in relation to their stand. This form must be returned before they arrive to set up their stand.

### Clear directions/map
Easy to read and accurate. The directions should include location of loading bays and details of whether vehicles will be required to move to a particular parking area after unloading.

### Details of what to do on arrival
Who to inform of their arrival. Include set-up times and dismantling times.

### Delivery instructions
Details of where and when deliveries can be made before the event and from where collections can be made after the event. This should include details of names, departments, etc that should be clearly marked on packages. The venue staff will be able to advise you on this.

### Details of lunch/hotel accommodation
Whether lunch/refreshments will be available for exhibitors and at what cost if not complimentary.

### Contact number for appropriate suppliers
Itemise exactly what will be available to them in terms of furniture – tables, chairs, power points, etc – and give details of suppliers who can provide additional items.

*Parking pass*
If applicable.

*Contact details for queries*
Details of how and when exhibitors can reach you, including on-site.

*A feedback form*
The opinion as to the success of the event is important from the exhibitors' point of view as well as the delegates' and speakers', so give them an opportunity to be constructively critical and to relate their own experiences and suggest new topics for future events.

## MAKING IT WORTHWHILE FOR EXHIBITORS

Conference exhibitors do not expect to have the attention of the delegates throughout the whole event, but to make it worth their while attending you must ensure that the delegates get to see them at every opportunity. Refreshment breaks and the lunch period are the most obvious. Refreshments should be taken in the exhibition area so delegates are not drawn away from the exhibition. Nibbles and sweet treats placed on the stands will help to encourage the delegates to visit the stands. Perhaps you could serve a finger buffet in the exhibition area and have dishes of scrumptious cakes and pastries on the stands for dessert.

Delegates tend to disappear quickly at the end of the day, so if you wish to encourage them to stay and view the stands again give them some encouragement in terms of food and drink. You may be thinking that all delegates do is eat and drink all day... but in fact, they do! It is part of the whole conference ethos and as an organiser you will naturally segregate your day into feeding times.

## Drawing attention to exhibitors

Instruct the chairperson to announce to the delegates when the exhibition will be open to them so that they have the opportunity to plan their visits to the stands. It will also help if you can spare a few minutes in the programme for a representative of each exhibiting company to introduce their company to the audience. Maximum use can then be made of the time available when delegates visit the stands. Just a couple of minutes each will suffice and help to make the exhibitors feel part of the event.

$$\left(12\right)$$

# The Morning After

*'After the event is the time to analyse the conference and your own performance.'*

## WINDING DOWN

After the busy period arranging and running the conference, it can be easy to lose the impetus to see the event through to the final stage. However, the days and weeks afterwards are very important as it is a time to analyse the conference and your own performance.

Ask yourself the following questions:

1. Did the conference satisfy the needs of the delegates?

2. Did the conference satisfy the needs of the organisers?

3. Did it serve its purpose?

4. Have the delegates taken on board what you wanted them to?

5. If they came to be educated, did they learn anything?

6. If they came to be informed, have they understood?

7. If they came to be entertained, have they gone away smiling?

8. Are the sponsors happy?

9. Are the exhibitors happy?

Newly formed relationships with delegates and sponsors can also now be consolidated, and post-event press coverage may be able to be obtained (see Chapter 10). Ensure that delegate details are passed on to those who may require them, such as sales and marketing departments, membership secretaries, etc, ensuring that data is strictly handled in accordance with data protection legislation.

## DEVELOPING RELATIONSHIPS

Ensure you follow through any requests made by delegates during the conference. In readiness for this make sure that you take a full note of any requests at the time and put them somewhere safe where you are going to be able to find them again. A book specifically for this purpose is worthwhile.

Respond to any other queries that may follow promptly and courteously.

### Remembering the speakers

Write to the speakers to thank them for their time and include payment for their services, expenses, etc if appropriate. Remember that the satisfaction, or not, of the delegates is largely in their hands and if it has worked out well they deserve to know about it. If you have used evaluation forms do pass on quotes to the speakers who may find them useful to use on other occasions.

### Remembering the sponsors

Your agreement with your sponsors may have included a copy of the delegate contact details. If this is so, send them out promptly so that the company concerned can use them to their best advantage. Again, bear in mind data protection legislation.

## EVALUATING THE EVENT

Don't be afraid to ask delegates for their opinions on the event. By asking them to complete a simple evaluation form at the end of the conference you can gather much useful information for future events, as well as obtaining their thoughts on your efforts this time around. The questionnaires can help you to make a judgement on the standard of venue, catering, booking arrangements, quality of presentations in content and delivery as well as obtaining suggestions for future events. See the example in Figure 19.

### Designing an evaluation form

Include an easy to complete evaluation form in the delegate packs. Ask the chairperson to highlight their presence as you have a much greater chance of having a substantial and worthwhile number returned whilst still on site than posted or faxed back after they have returned home. Most delegates will be happy to take a few minutes to complete the form, after all it is in their best interests to do so as its purpose is to understand the needs of the delegates better for future events.

The use of tick boxes or a simple marking system wherever possible enables swift completion of the form. You may wish to include a grading system for each of the speakers, based on delivery and content. This can be particularly useful for future events, and speakers who have scored well are able to refer to it when being considered for other events.

Diving for All Conference 200X

In order to provide the best possible service to our delegates, we would be very grateful if you would take a few minutes of your time today to fill in the following questionnaire. Please leave it in the questionnaire box by the desk or if you pre-fer fax (0234 45678) or post it back to us at Diving Today, PO Box 00, Bristol BS1 2UU.

1) Have you attended a Diving Today conference before? Yes / No

2) Did you learn of this one from (*please circle*)

Mailshot          Press          Word of mouth          WWW          Other

3) How would you grade the catering facilities at the venue? (*please circle*)

Poor          Adequate          Comfortable          Excellent

4) How would you grade the facilities at the venue? (*please circle*)

Poor          Average          Good          Excellent

5) Would you like to see future events held in (*please circle*)

Midlands          South          London          North          Scotland

6) Do you have any particular comments about this year's speaker programme?

7) Do you have any particular speakers in the UK or overseas you would like to hear at future events?

8) Are there any particular subject areas you would like to see covered at future events?

Thank you for your time.

Fig. 19. Evaluation form.

You may wish to include the delegates' names and contact details, or you could make the forms anonymous (thus encouraging delegates to be rather more candid).

### Professional research companies

Pre-event, on-site and post-event research can be undertaken on your behalf by professional marketing research companies using a variety of research methods. During the conference sophisticated and user-friendly terminals can be used that the delegates will be able to operate independently. Very useful data can be generated, and questions can also be included in the surveys on behalf of exhibitors, sponsors, etc. Professional reports will be provided that can be used to entice next year's exhibitors and delegates. An added benefit is that the research is seen to be unbiased as it is compiled externally. Specialist research companies advertise in trade journals and at trade exhibitions.

## WHERE TO GO FROM HERE

Firstly, give yourself a pat on the back. Remember that everyone has different ideals and that to keep the entire range of people – from speakers, venue staff, delegates and the rest of your organisation – happy is no mean feat. As said in Chapter 1, a seamless event belies the amount of time and effort that will have been put in. All those who have contributed to its success should be made aware of the value of their input, and to this end a letter of thanks to them and/or their respective managers would be appreciated.

As a final thought, give some consideration to the following questions, and make a note of your answers while the subject is still fresh in your mind.

1. Are there things that you would do differently next time?

2. Are there alternative types of venue that would have been more suitable?

3. Did anything occur that you were not prepared for?

You will now be in an excellent position to run your next event. Reflect on what you have achieved since you began the project, the people who you have come into contact with. Ready to start again?

# Appendix 1 –
# Data Protection

## DATA PROTECTION ACT 1998 AND ITS IMPLICATION ON THE CONFERENCE INDUSTRY

The Data Protection Act 1998 has distinct implications for the conference organiser. The Information Commissioner's office is very helpful in confirming exactly what you can and cannot do, and a free video is available explaining the main principles. They also have a comprehensive website at www.informationcommissioner.gov.uk

The eight principles put in place by the Data Protection Act 1998 to ensure information is handled properly are: That data must be:

1. fairly and lawfully processed;
2. processed for limited purposes;
3. adequate, relevant and not excessive;
4. accurate;
5. not kept for longer than is necessary;
6. processed in line with your rights;
7. secure; and
8. not transferred to countries without adequate protection.

By law 'data controllers' have to keep to these principles.

The data controller is 'A person who determines the purposes for which, and the manner in which, personal data are, or are to be, processed. This may be an individual or an organisation, and the processing may be carried out jointly or in common with other persons.'

The Data Protection Act has implications for all types of activities of any business or organisation. With respect to conference organisers, the main issues to consider are the storage and use of personal information provided by attendees.

This is particularly pertinent if the delegate is self employed, a sole trader or a partnership, where their personal and company details may be the same.

Delegates must be informed that their details will be held on your database. Although there may be emergency situations where details need to be shared, i.e. with the emergency services, in general if you have any intention of passing personal details on to anyone else, their permission must be granted. The following two paragraphs are examples of how these issues can be addressed on your booking form:

**a) Data protection policy:** The personal information provided by you will be held on the database of Interface Event Management & PR Ltd. If you wish to be informed of future events, please tick the box: ☐
The information will not be provided to third parties.

**b) Data protection policy:** The personal information provided by you will be held on the database of Interface

Event Management & PR Ltd. If you would like to be informed of future events, please tick this box: ☐ If you would like to be contacted by specially selected third parties with similar information, please tick this box: ☐

# Appendix 2 –
# Health and Safety

You are morally, legally and ethically obliged to ensure that everyone attending your conference will be safe. Organisers can be held responsible in cases of litigation and the penalties are severe. A thorough risk assessment should therefore be carried out in relation to the event.

## CARRYING OUT THE RISK ASSESSMENT

You can do this yourself and advice can be obtained from your local Health and Safety Inspector. The Health and Safety Executive suggest **Five Steps to Risk Assessment**.

### Step 1: Look for the hazards

A hazard is anything that can cause harm. Consider the venue, its physical surroundings, the staging and sets. Walk around the entire area where delegates, contractors, staff or speakers may have access.

### Step 2: Decide who might be harmed and how

Consider everyone involved in the conference and how the hazards identified above could affect them.

### Step 3: Evaluate

Evaluate the risks and decide whether the existing precautions are adequate or whether more should be done. A risk is the chance that somebody will be harmed by the hazard. How likely is it that each of the hazards identified in Step 1 could cause harm? Consider whether anything can be done to reduce the risk, to make it as low as possible. For example, if there is a step beyond a doorway that is not expected by someone walking through, a clear notice warning of it before the doorway will reduce the risk of someone falling down it. Although hazards may not be able to be completely eliminated, they can then be graded as being high, medium or low risk. Ask yourself these questions:

1. Can I get rid of the hazard completely?

2. If not, how can I control the risks?
   – try a less risky option if one is available
   – prevent access to the hazard
   – issue personal protective clothing/insist on
     contractors wearing necessary protective clothing.

**Step 4: Record your findings**
Keep a written record in your conference file and update it as necessary. In the instance of an investigation being made after an incident, the written audit trail will be vital evidence. A simple chart as in Figure 20 will also act as a prompt to ensure that the risk assessment has been completed. The chart should show that a proper check was made, by whom and when, that the outcome was that hazards were identified, people at risk were identified and that precautions have been taken to ensure risk is low.

## Step 5: Review your assessment and revise if necessary

The level of risk and opportunities for hazards can alter as your conference progresses. Hazards may be present during the set-up day that are not present during the conference itself. Conversely the exhibition could add hazards that were not there before (see Chapter 12 – Exhibitors). It is vital then that the risk assessment is updated as significant changes occur. Also establish whether the venue has its own Health and Safety regulations that must be adhered to. Request these in writing and ensure they are built into your overall plan.

## GETTING FURTHER GUIDANCE

The Health and Safety Executive publish a number of guidebooks to help you understand risk assessment and the legal requirements involved. Details can be obtained from: HSE Order Line: 01787 881165. The Five Step plan above is adapted from the HSE's publication *Five Steps to Risk Assessment.**

Event title: *The Ages of Man*   Date of event: *24th March 200X*

Organisation: College of Human Sciences   Venue: *Tropador Museum*

Names of key personnel:   *Polly Marston (Organiser)*
*Emily Marcus (Assistant to PM)*
*Anita Cork (Director - CHS)*

Date of assessment: *12th March 200X* Updated on: *23rd March 200X*

Assessment carried out by: *Polly Marston*

| Hazards Identified | Level of Risk | People at Risk | Control/Action | Update/Notes |
|---|---|---|---|---|
| *Electrical tools during exhibition set-up* | *Medium* | *Exhibitors, other contractors* | *Ensure users are trained in their use. No such equipment is to be left unattended with a live power supply to it* | *Draw to attention of venue management* |
| *Step down into gents toilet block easily missed* | *High* | *All person entering the toilet block* | *Stick a thick line of contrasting tape along the edge of the step. Place warning sign at each side of the entrance* | *Check all cabling before delegates are given access.* |
| *Injury from items related to exhibition break-down at end of conference* | *Medium* | *All persons in immediate vicinity* | *Make sure exhibitors are issued with instructions not to break down their stands until all delegates have left the exhibition hall* | |
| *Electrical and other cables in use by exhibitors, technicians etc* | *High* | *All persons in locality* | *Trailing cables should be kept to a minimum and in protective sheaths. All to be taped down and secure and not trailing across walkways* | |

| Fire evacuation procedure established | Details issued to Chairperson | Details announced to attendees | Notes |
|---|---|---|---|
| *Exits identified/ meeting place in safe area located as per instructions from venue* | *24th March* | *During Opening remarks 24/3.19X* | *Briefing to all staff/ exhibitors not attending conference carried out by PM* |

Fig. 20. Risk assessment form.

# Appendix 3 – First Aid

The Health and Safety (First Aid) Regulations 1981 require that first aid equipment, facilities and personnel trained in their use are provided in all places of work. This does not specifically include conferences, however the Health and Safety At Work Act 1974 requires that individuals have a duty of care to people who may enter our places of work. These may include conference delegates and contractors, but if there is any doubt it is better to err on the side of caution and have safety procedures in place as a matter of course and conduct a first aid assessment.

According to the Health and Safety Executive, what is considered adequate and appropriate will depend on the circumstances. As a guide the minimum first aid provision on any work site is:

◆ a suitably stocked first aid box
◆ an appointed person to take charge of first aid arrangements.

An appointed person is someone who takes charge when someone falls ill, including calling an ambulance if required. The person should be available at all times, but should not attempt to give first aid for which they have not been trained. At all conferences there should be at least one qualified first-aider present, preferably one for every 50 delegates. A first-aider is someone who has undergone and holds a certificate from a HSE approved training course in first aid at work. The first-aider can also be the appointed person.

## SUGGESTED MINIMUM REQUIREMENTS OF A FIRST AID BOX

◆ Twenty individually wrapped sterile adhesive dressings.
◆ Two sterile eye pads.
◆ Four individually wrapped triangular bandages.
◆ Six safety pins.
◆ Six medium-sized individually wrapped sterile unmedicated wound dressings.
◆ One pair of disposable gloves.

This information is taken from the excellent and very useful Health and Safety Executive website. It contains question and answer pages, details of local contact numbers for enquiries, HSE statistics and an A–Z of relevant subjects. The site can be found at www.hse.gov.uk/index.htm There is also an HSE InfoLine on 0845 3450055.

# Appendix 4 –
# Booking Forms

As discussed in Chapter 4, the layout and design of the conference brochure are very important, it must not only look good, it must 'work'. Correct layout will ensure that when the delegate tears off and returns the booking form, essential information is not lost to them. The following diagrams (i) a suggested layout for a fairly simple booking system, and (ii) a more detailed example of the booking form section where various payment methods are included.

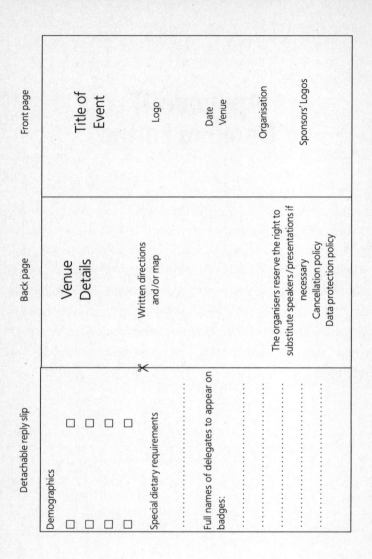

A simple booking form.

Inside front cover

Programme

Detachable reply slip

## Booking form
Title of Event

Name:
Address:

Tel:        Fax:        Email:

I would like to book _ ticket(s)
to attend the conference at

☐ £xx (Early Bird price)
  postmarked before xx/xx/xx

☐ £xx Standard price
  postmarked on or after
  xx/xx/xx

Please make cheques payable to
  Your company

Post to: Your name, Your company,
  Your address, Your fax number

Telephone no for enquiries (01234)
56789

Add credit card payment area if applicable

*Please complete both sides of form*

Web address

Time
Title of Presentation
Name of Speaker

Text

– Description
of
Event

# Booking form

Name............................

Postition ..........................     Organisation ...................

Address: ...........................................................

..........................................................................

..................................     Postcode ......................

Telephone.................     Fax .............     Email................

Special dietary or access requirements ...................................

**Payment method**

Cheque enclosed ☐        Credit card ☐
*(payable to XXXX)*        *(Visa/Mastercard/Delta)*

Credit card number.................     Expiry date.....................

Security number ...................

Name of cardholder as printed on card       ..............................

Cardholder's billing address (*if different from above*).....................

..........................................................................

..........................................................................

Signature.........................     Total payment .................

Post or fax your booking form to: Your Name, Your Company, Your Address, Your Postcode. Tel: (0123) 456789 Fax: (0123) 987654

Registration fees:      Early Bird booking price £75 plus Vat
(postmarked before 11/05/00)

Standard booking price £85 plus Vat
(postmarked on or after 12/05/00)

Registration fee includes buffet lunch, tea and coffee, conference session and speaker papers where available.

**Cancellation policy:** A refund will be given if the cancellation is received on or before 14 days prior to the event. Cancellations within 14 days of the event will not receive a refund. Please submit your cancellation in writing by e-mail, fax or post. Substitutions can be made at any time.

**Data protection policy:** The personal information provided by you will be held on the database of the APBC, c/o Interface Event Management & PR Ltd. The information will not be provided to third parties. If you would like to be informed of future events, please tick the box ☐.

A more complex booking form.

# Appendix 5 –
# Banquets/Conference Dinners

Many conferences incorporate a dinner for delegates, speakers and guests. Here are a few hints and tips you may find useful to set you on the right track.

Consult freely with the banqueting manager at your chosen venue. He/she will have extensive experience in producing events and will know what works well for their particular facility. This includes; turnaround time if the room is to be in use during the day, layout, chef specialities, etc.

To ensure your event runs smoothly, consider employing the services of a professional toastmaster (visit www.natuk.com). These gentlemen (and ladies!) are supremely versed in protocol and etiquette and will readily discuss your plans with you. They will introduce VIP guests, after-dinner speakers and make any housekeeping announcements required and generally provide a guiding and coordinating hand. Additionally they have much experience in dealing with loud and merry guests in a tactful but effective manner. Dressed in their splendid uniform, the toastmaster can make an occasion a rather more grand affair. If you do not feel that a toastmaster is appropriate for your event, the banqueting manager may take on the role to a limited extent. Make sure that whoever is used they are fully briefed with the running order and speaker biographies. Remember you may need to arrange for a microphone/amplification and possibly even spotlights for your speakers.

To avoid congestion around table plans, produce an alphabetical list of guests listed with their allotted table number. Staff can be on hand with copies ready to mingle with the guests and ensure that everyone knows where to sit. Alternatively and if you are working with a manage-able number, the table plan could be printed on the evening's programme if there is one.

### Room dressing

Table decorations can take the form of candles, floral arrangements, balloons or a mixture of these three. If you are being really extravagant you could use ice sculptures or chocolate fountains! If the conference or organisation has its own corporate colours, these can be incorporated into the decorations to make it look particularly stylish and professional.

**Candles:** check the health and safety policy of the venue. Some only allow floating candles, tea lights in holders or no naked flames at all.

**Balloons** tend to be cheaper than flowers and can provide height as well as colour. Matching pillars and archways can be produced for the stage and entrances.

**Floral arrangements** are better low or tall and thin so that they do not impede the view of the diners across the table.

## Menus

Menus offer an opportunity for sponsorship, and carry the conference logo, title and sponsor details if required, as well as the menu and order of speeches, etc. If the venue is producing standard menus on your behalf, proof-read them prior to the guests arriving. Typos and grammatical errors can creep in anywhere!

Ensure that guests have the opportunity to declare special dietary requirements in advance and that the information is forwarded to the venue in good time. The chef will need to be aware of vegetarian, vegan, diabetic, gluten free, kosher, etc requests several days in advance. It is also helpful to indicate to the waiting staff where the guests needing special diets are to be seated.

Should the vegetarian selection be listed on the menu? As a vegetarian myself I like to see it listed, but there is a danger that a large number of guests who have not previously declared themselves vegetarian will suddenly become a vegetarian for the night, having decided their option is more appetising than the standard dish. Again, seek advice from the banqueting manager as to how flexible the chef can be.

## Drinks

Check that the space provide for pre-dinner drinks is adequate for the number of invited guests and that cloakroom facilities are provided.

If you are expecting your dinner guests to arrive all at the same time, for example if you are bringing delegates to the venue by coach, ensure the banqueting manager is aware so that staff can be prepared for everyone to descend on the bar at once. To prevent queues and if your budget allows, provide a welcome drink served from trays or serving stations around the room.

If running an account bar (where all the charges go back to the main account) provide vouchers for your guests so that additional charges cannot be added without your knowledge.

As an average, half a bottle of wine per person is often included with the meal. It is also standard practice to provide still and sparkling bottled water. Make sure all bottles are put onto the tables to prevent being charged for any not consumed.

### After-dinner entertainment
The options are endless, particularly if you have a significant budget available. You can expect to pay between £1,000 and £25,000 for a celebrity after-dinner speaker booked through an agency. Also allow for additional costs such as travel expenditure, accommodation and any personal requirements listed on their rider (list of 'necessary' requirements) which can seriously increase the costs. Obviously this expenditure can be significantly reduced if using an entertaining industry personality, etc or someone else appropriately connected to your organisation.

# Index

accommodation, 23, 35, 47, 48
acoustics, 18, 78
audio visual, 14, 18, 24, 34, 47, 48, 62, 74, 81, 84, 90

badge, 46, 52, 56, 58, 73, 85, 86
banquets, 17, 127
break even, 63
brochure, 10, 11, 38, 44, 48, 61, 73, 114
budget, 6, 9, 44, 48, 60, 99

call for papers, 27
catering, 22, 64, 66, 90
chair person, 34, 37, 90, 92, 107
communication, 1, 3
computer generated graphics, 75
conference dinners, 17, 127

data protection, 40, 73, 114
delegate packs, 15, 47, 87

exhibitions, 5, 20, 21, 100
exhibitor packs, 104
evaluation form, 109, 110, 111

first aid, 121
fixed costs, 60
floorplan, 103

'graveyard slot', 50

health and safety, 20, 92, 105, 117

income, 61, 101
insurance, 64

journalists, 98

lectern, 19, 24, 68, 80
local conference bureaux, 12
local newspapers, 94
local radio, 96

media, 98

Members of Parliament, 28
menus, 129
microphones, 18, 24, 79

negotiating, 24, 67

overhead projection, 74, 78
overlap, 32
overseas speakers, 33

press coverage, 94
press release, 47, 96
press room, 98
printing, 42
professionals, 2, 68
programme, 43, 44, 46

questionnaire, 25

registration, 52, 58, 85
rehearsal, 30
risk assessment, 117

scheduling, 44
shell scheme, 102, 103
slide projection, 76, 77

software, 12, 52
sound systems, 78
sourcing speakers, 25
speaker bureaux, 28
speaker care, 91
speaker information packs, 33
speakers, 25, 91, 109
sponsorship, 35, 46, 55, 60, 68, 69, 81, 86, 87, 109
staff, 83
staging the event, 83

time plan, 45, 47, 48
tool box, 92
trouble-shooting, 93

universities, 9

value added tax (VAT), 63
variable costs, 61, 62
venue, 8
venue-finding options, 11
video projection, 75

web-based registration, 53